Microsoft

MOS 2013 Study Guide
for Microsoft Access

John Pierce

Contents

What do you think of this book? We want to hear from you!

Microsoft is interested in hearing your feedback so we can continually improve our books and learning resources for you. To participate in a brief online survey, please visit:

microsoft.com/learning/booksurvey

3   Create queries   95

4   Create forms   129

5   Create reports   171

Introduction

The Microsoft Office Specialist (MOS) certification program has been designed to validate your knowledge of and ability to use programs in the Microsoft Office 2013 suite of programs, Microsoft Office 365, and Microsoft SharePoint. This book has been designed to guide you in studying the types of tasks you are likely to be required to demonstrate in Exam 77-424: Microsoft Access 2013.

Who this book is for

MOS 2013 Study Guide for Microsoft Access is designed for experienced computer users seeking Microsoft Office Specialist certification in Access 2013.

MOS exams for individual programs are practical rather than theoretical. You must demonstrate that you can complete certain tasks or projects rather than simply answering questions about program features. The successful MOS certification candidate will have at least six months of experience using all aspects of the application on a regular basis, for example, using Access at work or school to create and manage databases, build database tables, import and export data, design and run queries, create and format forms, and design detail and summary reports.

As a certification candidate, you probably have a lot of experience with the program you want to become certified in. Many of the procedures described in this book will be familiar to you; others might not be. Read through each study section and ensure that you are familiar with not only the procedures included in the section, but also the concepts and tools discussed in the review information. In some cases, graphics depict the tools you will use to perform procedures related to the skill set. Study the graphics and ensure that you are familiar with all the options available for each tool.

How this book is organized

The exam coverage is divided into chapters representing broad skill sets that correlate to the functional groups covered by the exam, and each chapter is divided into sections addressing groups of related skills that correlate to the exam objectives. Each section includes review information, generic procedures, and practice tasks you can complete on your own while studying. When necessary, we provide practice files you can use to work through the practice tasks. You can practice the procedures in this book by using the practice files supplied or by using your own files. (If you use your own files, keep in mind that functionality in Access 2013 is limited in files created in or saved for earlier versions of the program.)

Download the practice files

Before you can complete the exercises in this book, you need to download the book's practice files to your computer. These practice files can be downloaded from the following page:

http://aka.ms/mosAccess2013/files

> **Important** The Access 2013 program is not available from this website. You should purchase and install that program before using this book.

If you would like to be able to refer to the completed versions of practice files at a later time, you can save the practice files that you modify while working through the exercises in this book. If you save your changes and later want to repeat the exercise, you can download the original practice files again.

The following table lists the practice files for this book.

Folder and functional group	Files
MOSAccess2013\Objective1 1 Create and manage databases	Marketing_1.accdb
MOSAccess2013\Objective2 2 Build tables	Employees.accdb Marketing_2.accdb Northwind.accdb Tasks.txt
MOSAccess2013\Objective3 3 Create queries	Marketing_3.accdb
MOSAccess2013\Objective4 4 Create forms	Marketing_4.accdb
MOSAccess2013\Objective5 5 Create reports	Marketing_5.accdb

Adapting exercise steps

The screen images shown in this book were captured at a screen resolution of 1024 × 768, at 100 percent magnification. If your settings are different, the ribbon on your screen might not look the same as the one shown in this book. For example, you might have more or fewer buttons in each of the groups, the buttons you have might be represented by larger or smaller icons than those shown, or the group might be represented by a button that you click to display the group's commands. As a result, exercise instructions that involve the ribbon might require a little adaptation. Our instructions use this format:

→ On the **Insert** tab, in the **Illustrations** group, click the **Chart** button.

If the command is in a list or on a menu, our instructions use this format:

→ On the **Home** tab, in the **Editing** group, click the **Find** arrow and then, on the **Find** menu, click **Advanced Find**.

> **Tip** On subsequent instances of instructions located on the same tab or in the same group, the instructions are simplified to reflect that we've already established the working location.

If differences between your display settings and ours cause a button to appear differently on your screen than it does in this book, you can easily adapt the steps to locate the command. First click the specified tab, and then locate the specified group. If a group has been collapsed into a group list or under a group button, click the list or button to display the group's commands. If you can't immediately identify the button you want, point to likely candidates to display their names in ScreenTips.

If you prefer not to have to adapt the steps, set up your screen to match ours while you read and work through the exercises in this book.

In this book, we provide instructions based on the traditional keyboard and mouse input methods. If you're using the program on a touch-enabled device, you might be giving commands by tapping with a stylus or your finger. If so, substitute a tapping action any time we instruct you to click a user interface element. Also note that when we tell you to enter information, you can do so by typing on a keyboard, tapping an on-screen keyboard, or even speaking aloud, depending on your computer setup and your personal preferences.

Ebook edition

If you're reading the ebook edition of this book, you can do the following:

- Search the full text
- Print
- Copy and paste

You can purchase and download the ebook edition from our Microsoft Press site at oreilly.com, which you can find at:

http://aka.ms/mosAccess2013

Get support and give feedback

The following sections provide information about getting help with this book and contacting us to provide feedback or report errors.

Errata

We've made every effort to ensure the accuracy of this book and its companion content. Any errors that have been reported since this book was published are listed on our Microsoft Press site, which you can find at:

http://aka.ms/mosAccess2013/errata

If you find an error that is not already listed, you can report it to us through the same page.

If you need additional support, email Microsoft Press Book Support at:

mspinput@microsoft.com

Please note that product support for Microsoft software is not offered through the preceding addresses.

We want to hear from you

At Microsoft Press, your satisfaction is our top priority, and your feedback our most valuable asset. Please tell us what you think of this book at:

http://www.microsoft.com/learning/booksurvey

The survey is short, and we read every one of your comments and ideas. Thanks in advance for your input!

Stay in touch

Let's keep the conversation going! We're on Twitter at:

http://twitter.com/MicrosoftPress

Taking a Microsoft Office Specialist exam

Desktop computing proficiency is increasingly important in today's business world. When screening, hiring, and training employees, employers can feel reassured by relying on the objectivity and consistency of technology certification to ensure the competence of their workforce. As an employee or job seeker, you can use technology certification to prove that you already have the skills you need to succeed, saving current and future employers the time and expense of training you.

Microsoft Office Specialist certification

Microsoft Office Specialist certification is designed to assist employees in validating their skills with Office programs. The following certification paths are available:

- A Microsoft Office Specialist (MOS) is an individual who has demonstrated proficiency by passing a certification exam in one or more Office programs, including Microsoft Word, Excel, PowerPoint, Outlook, Access, OneNote, or SharePoint.

- A Microsoft Office Specialist Expert (MOS Expert) is an individual who has taken his or her knowledge of Office to the next level and has demonstrated by passing a certification exam that he or she has mastered the more advanced features of Word or Excel.

Selecting a certification path

When deciding which certifications you would like to pursue, you should assess the following:

- The program and program version(s) with which you are familiar
- The length of time you have used the program and how frequently you use it
- Whether you have had formal or informal training in the use of that program
- Whether you use most or all of the available program features
- Whether you are considered a go-to resource by business associates, friends, and family members who have difficulty with the program

Candidates for MOS-level certification are expected to successfully complete a wide range of standard business tasks, such as formatting a document or worksheet and its content; creating and formatting visual content; or working with SharePoint lists, libraries, Web Parts, and dashboards. Successful candidates generally have six or more months of experience with the specific Office program, including either formal, instructor-led training or self-study using MOS-approved books, guides, or interactive computer-based materials.

Candidates for MOS Expert–level certification are expected to successfully complete more complex tasks that involve using the advanced functionality of the program. Successful candidates generally have at least six months, and may have several years, of experience with the programs, including formal, instructor-led training or self-study using MOS-approved materials.

Test-taking tips

Every MOS certification exam is developed from a set of exam skill standards (referred to as the objective domain) that are derived from studies of how the Office programs are used in the workplace. Because these skill standards dictate the scope of each exam, they provide critical information about how to prepare for certification. This book follows the structure of the published exam objectives; see "How this book is organized" in the Introduction for more information.

The MOS certification exams are performance based and require you to complete business-related tasks or projects in the program for which you are seeking certification. For example, you might be presented with a file and told to do something specific with it, or presented with a sample document and told to create it by using resources provided for that purpose. Your score on the exam reflects how well you perform the requested tasks or complete the project within the allotted time.

Here is some helpful information about taking the exam:

- Keep track of the time. Your exam time does not officially begin until after you finish reading the instructions provided at the beginning of the exam. During the exam, the amount of time remaining is shown at the bottom of the exam interface. You can't pause the exam after you start it.

- Pace yourself. At the beginning of the exam, you will receive information about the questions or projects that are included in the exam. Some questions will require that you complete more than one task. Each project will require that you complete multiple tasks. During the exam, the amount of time remaining to complete the questions or project, and the number of completed and remaining questions if applicable, is shown at the bottom of the exam interface.

- Read the exam instructions carefully before beginning. Follow all the instructions provided completely and accurately.

- Enter requested information as it appears in the instructions, but without duplicating the formatting unless you are specifically instructed to do so. For example, the text and values you are asked to enter might appear in the instructions in bold and underlined text, but you should enter the information without applying these formats.

- Close all dialog boxes before proceeding to the next exam question unless you are specifically instructed not to do so.

- Don't close task panes before proceeding to the next exam question unless you are specifically instructed to do so.

- If you are asked to print a document, worksheet, chart, report, or slide, perform the task, but be aware that nothing will actually be printed.

- When performing tasks to complete a project-based exam, save your work frequently.

- Don't worry about extra keystrokes or mouse clicks. Your work is scored based on its result, not on the method you use to achieve that result (unless a specific method is indicated in the instructions).

- If a computer problem occurs during the exam (for example, if the exam does not respond or the mouse no longer functions) or if a power outage occurs, contact a testing center administrator immediately. The administrator will restart the computer and return the exam to the point where the interruption occurred, with your score intact.

Certification benefits

At the conclusion of the exam, you will receive a score report, indicating whether you passed the exam. If your score meets or exceeds the passing standard (the minimum required score), you will be contacted by email by the Microsoft Certification Program team. The email message you receive will include your Microsoft Certification ID and links to online resources, including the Microsoft Certified Professional site. On this site, you can download or order a printed certificate, create a virtual business card, order an ID card, view and share your certification transcript, access the Logo Builder, and access other useful and interesting resources, including special offers from Microsoft and affiliated companies.

Depending on the level of certification you achieve, you will qualify to display one of three logos on your business card and other personal promotional materials. These logos attest to the fact that you are proficient in the applications or cross-application skills necessary to achieve the certification.

Microsoft Microsoft Microsoft
Office Specialist   Office Specialist Expert   Office Specialist Master

Using the Logo Builder, you can create a personalized certification logo that includes the MOS logo and the specific programs in which you have achieved certification. If you achieve MOS certification in multiple programs, you can include multiple certifications in one logo.

For more information

To learn more about the Microsoft Office Specialist exams and related courseware, visit:

http://www.microsoft.com/learning/en/us/mos-certification.aspx

Microsoft Access 2013

This book covers the skills you need to have for certification as a Microsoft Office Specialist in Microsoft Access 2013. Specifically, you need to be able to complete tasks that demonstrate the following skill sets:

1 Create and manage databases
2 Build tables
3 Create queries
4 Create forms
5 Create reports

With these skills, you can create, populate, and manage the types of databases most commonly used in a business environment.

Prerequisites

We assume that you have been working with Access 2013 for at least six months and that you know how to carry out fundamental tasks that are not specifically mentioned in the objectives for this Microsoft Office Specialist exam.

The certification exam and the content of this book address the processes of designing and building Access databases. We assume that you are familiar with the Microsoft Office ribbon and that you understand basic Access features—for example, that you know how to enter and edit data. We also assume you are familiar with the definition and function of relational databases and database objects such as tables and forms. To provide context and an opportunity for review, the following list provides brief explanations of five important terms.

- **Relationship** Helps maintain the integrity of the information in a database and also reduce data redundancy. You can create several types of relationships between tables in an Access database. In a one-to-many relationship, a record in one table can be related to one or many records in another. You can also create one-to-one relationships and many-to-many relationships. Relationships are created by linking a table's foreign key (a customer ID field in an order table) with another table's primary key (the customer ID field in the customer table). Relationships protect data integrity by preventing you from creating orphan records (for example, an order with no customer). Relationships help reduce data redundancy by letting you store information in separate tables that you link together. For example, you can create a customer table and then relate each order in an order table to the record for a particular customer. This prevents you from having to enter a custom record for each separate order.

- **Table** Defines the data stored in a database. Tables are composed of fields, and each field is defined as a particular data type (text, number, date, or another data type). Each field also has certain properties. For example, you can specify that a field is required. You can also define the size of a field (such as the maximum number of characters a field can contain). Users of a database fill in fields (and must fill in required fields) with values to create a record in the database. In most tables, each record is identified by a unique value called a *primary key*, which might be a single field (such as a product ID) or a combination of fields.

- **Query** Can be used to select records that meet specific criteria and to perform actions such as updating a group of records. To build a select query, you add fields from one or more tables and then define criteria that Access uses to retrieve the records you want to view. For example, you might want to retrieve records with a certain value in a date field (all records created after 1/1/2014, for example) or records associated with a specific project. Using criteria, you can also create and run action queries that insert, update, or delete selected records.

- **Form** Used to display, enter, and edit data. Forms are often bound to tables (or to queries) as a record source. Forms use controls such as text boxes, check boxes, and list boxes to provide a user interface for a database. Forms can also be used to confirm and execute database operations and to navigate from one database object to another. Access provides several built-in form designs, a gallery of form controls, and tools you use to design and lay out a form.

- **Report** Used to share and present data and to summarize data for a specific field or fields. You might print reports for a meeting or distribute them electronically as a PDF file or in email.

1 Create and manage databases

The skills tested in this section of the Microsoft Office Specialist exam for Microsoft Access 2013 relate to creating and managing databases. Specifically, the following objectives are associated with this set of skills:

1.1 Create new databases

1.2 Manage relationships and keys

1.3 Navigate through databases

1.4 Protect and maintain databases

1.5 Print and export databases

Many of the operations and tasks involved in creating and managing Access databases originate in the Backstage view. The New page presents many templates that you can use to create a database and a search box that lets you locate other templates. You can use the Save As page to back up a database and to save a database in a file format that's compatible with an earlier version of Access. The Info page provides commands that help you maintain and secure a database.

This chapter guides you in studying how to perform these operations and describes other important concepts and techniques involved in creating and managing an Access database—how to set and manage relationships between Access tables, how to navigate through a database, and how to export the data you store in Access to other programs and to other formats.

> **Practice Files** To complete the practice tasks in this chapter, you need the practice files contained in the MOSAccess2013\Objective1 practice file folder. For more information, see "Download the practice files" in this book's Introduction.

1.1 Create new databases

When you start Access (provided that you don't open a database you've used recently or double-click a database file), the program opens to its startup screen. Along the left side of the window, Access displays a list of recent files and a link you can use to open other files. Most importantly, the startup screen displays a set of thumbnails for templates you can use to create a variety of desktop databases or Access web apps (a type of database stored in the cloud). In addition to the templates for specific types of databases, Access provides an option for creating a blank desktop database or a custom (blank) web app. The same template thumbnails are displayed on the New page in the Backstage view.

> **Tip** The templates shown by default include those for asset and issue tracking, project and task management, and contacts. For each category, a thumbnail is included for a desktop database and for an Access web app.

At the top of the window is the search box, with the prompt "Search for online templates," and just below the search box is an array of suggested search terms. Click one of the suggested search terms, or use the search box to locate other templates that might be available.

Access databases are made up of database objects, including tables, queries, forms, reports, and supporting objects (such as macros). Templates come with database objects in place. The Project Management desktop template, for example, includes tables that define records for common tasks (tasks that occur in more than one project), project details, and task definitions, and other tables. This template also includes several queries (such as one to view open projects); forms for working with data such as project, employee, and task details; and several reports (such as Tasks By Assigned To).

> **Tip** Access 2013 includes the Northwind sample database, which has been part of Access for many versions of the program. The Northwind database provides examples of features, including a login dialog box, and sample macros and Microsoft Visual Basic for Application (VBA) modules. Use the search box to find the Northwind database (the thumbnail identifies the database as the Desktop Northwind 2007 Sample Database), and then refer to it when you're looking for a particular solution, or just work with it from time to time to gain an understanding of the extent of the work you can do in Access.

The following sections provide more details about creating a desktop database and an Access web app by using a template as your starting point. This section also describes the tools for creating tables, forms, and other objects when you start with a blank database; how to build and add to a database by using application parts; and how to create a database that uses an earlier Access file format.

Creating desktop databases

When you click a thumbnail for a desktop database template on the startup screen, Access displays a window that provides a description of the template and indicates the initial file size and a rating. (You can use the arrows that appear to the left and right of this window to browse through the set of templates.)

By default, Access names files by using Database*n*, where *n* is a number such as 1 or 2. Enter a descriptive name, and then click the folder icon to select a folder, other than the default Documents folder, in which to store the database file. When you click Create, Access prepares the template and opens the new database. (Depending on your security settings, you might need to click Enable Content in the Message Bar to work with VBA macros.)

In most cases, Access displays a default table or opens a form for data input. Along the left side of the window is the Access Navigation pane. If the Navigation pane is collapsed, click the chevron at the top of the pane to view the database objects included in this template.

> **See Also** For more information about how to view objects in the Navigation pane, see the "Configuring the Navigation pane" topic in section 1.3, "Navigate through databases."

A template is designed to provide each object and feature you need, but you can also create additional objects for the database. To create database objects, you work with options on the ribbon's Create tab, which includes command groups related to tables, queries, forms, reports, and macros and code modules. The Create tab is also the starting point for working with application parts.

> **See Also** For more information about application parts, see the "Working with application parts" topic later in this section.

> **Tip** If you base your database on a template, you can begin entering data by using one of the default tables and forms. You can also use commands in the Import & Link group on the External Data tab to import data into your database. For more information, see the "Importing data into a table" topic in section 2.1, "Create a table."

If you prefer to start from scratch and create your own desktop database, on the startup screen or the New page, click Blank Desktop Database. A blank database opens with the Navigation pane expanded. Access also creates a single default database object, called *Table1*, which serves as a starting point. (To give the table a more meaningful name, right-click Table1 in the Navigation pane, and then click Rename.) In a new blank database, Access also displays the field list, which is empty at this point. After you define fields for the tables in your database, you use the field list to add fields to queries, forms, and other database objects.

➤ To create a desktop database

1. On the startup screen or the **New** page, click a template thumbnail (use the search box to locate a template that's not displayed) or click **Blank desktop database**.

2. In the **File Name** box, enter a name for the database.

3. Click the folder icon to the right of the **File Name** box if you want to store the database in a location other than your **Documents** folder.

4. Click **Create**. Access prepares the template and opens the new database.

5. If the Message Bar appears with a security warning, click **Enable Content**.

Creating Access web apps

The steps to create an Access web app from a template are essentially the same as those for creating a desktop database. First, on the startup screen or the New page in the Backstage view, click a thumbnail (one that's displayed by default, a template you locate through a search, or the thumbnail for the custom web app). In the window that Access displays, enter a name for the app and then select a location from the Available Locations list. (You can also enter a URL in the Web Location box.) These locations are derived from Microsoft SharePoint sites associated with your Microsoft Office 365 account or on a SharePoint server at your organization.

Important Access Services must be enabled for the SharePoint site before you can save an Access web app to that location. In addition, you need Full permissions to a location to create a web app there. For more information, see "Overview of Access Services in SharePoint Server 2013" at *http://technet.microsoft.com/en-us/library/ee748634.aspx.*

After Access contacts the server and creates the app, Access displays the Add Tables window, with the template's default tables listed along the left side. To add another table to the web app, use the search box to locate a table template, or click the link provided to add a blank table. At the bottom of the Add Tables window are icons that you can use to create a table from other data sources, including another Access database, a Microsoft Excel workbook, a Microsoft SQL Server or Open Database Connectivity (ODBC) database, a text file (.txt or .csv), or a SharePoint list.

The web app template
creates these tables by default

Use these icons to import
data into the web app

Web apps are used mostly for adding and viewing data. You do the design work required to build a database in Access and not in your browser. On the pared-down ribbon that's displayed for a web app, you can display the Navigation pane, create a subset of database objects (tables, queries, views, and macros), and open the web app in your browser by clicking Launch App. Views are similar to forms in a desktop database. By default, Access creates List and Datasheet views for each table in a web app.

In your browser, after you update and add data, click the Settings button (the gear icon) in the upper-right corner, and then click Customize In Access to open the database in Access and make changes to its design. To save changes to your web app, click Save on the Quick Access Toolbar or on the File tab.

> **See Also** For more information about adding tables to an Access web app, see section 2.1, "Create a table." For more information about queries, see all sections of Chapter 3, "Create queries." For more information about web app views, see the "Creating views in an Access web app" topic in section 4.1, "Create a form."

➤ **To create an Access web app**

1. On the startup screen or the **New** page, click a template thumbnail for a web app (use the search box to locate a template that's not displayed), or click **Custom web app**.

2. In the **App Name** box, enter a name for the web app.

3. In the **Web Location** box, enter a URL for the site where you want to store the web app, or use the **Available Locations** list to specify the location.

4. Click **Create**.

Working with application parts

One of the ways in which you can incorporate tables, forms, and other objects into a database is by using an application part. An *application part* can be a single form (which is not yet bound to the records in any table or query) or a set of database objects (a table or two and related forms and reports, for example).

On the Create tab, click Application Parts (in the Templates group) to display the blank forms and Quick Start templates you can work with. The following sections cover the details of working with the different types of application parts.

> **Tip** As a step in creating a database template, you can create an application part. The templates you save appear in the Application Parts gallery, under the heading User Templates by default. You can define a different category when you save the template. For more information, see the "Saving databases as templates" topic in section 1.5, "Print and export databases."

Inserting blank forms

Each of the blank forms that Access provides as application parts comes with basic command button controls and design elements (a title, for example, and placeholders for fields and labels) that you build on to complete the form's design and layout. The command buttons that appear on application part forms are programmed to perform certain actions. For example, the Dialog form in the Application Parts gallery comes with a Save button and a Save & Close button. By default, the Save button saves the current record, and the Save & Close button saves the record and then closes the form. (You can replace the default action performed by a command button by assigning a different macro to the button's OnClick event.)

> **See Also** For information about creating a form and using form controls, see all sections in Chapter 4, "Create forms."

You can choose from several types of built-in blank forms. (Access displays a ScreenTip that briefly describes each blank form's layout and design).

- Single-column forms (1 Right and 1 Top) with labels to the right of the field names or above the field names.

- Two-column forms (2 Right and 2 Top) with labels to the right of the field names or above the field names.

- Details form, which is a single-record form with a subform that shows detailed records related to the record displayed in the main form.

- Dialog form that you can design as a dialog box and use to execute and confirm operations (such as saving a record).

- List form, which displays multiple items in a list format. The command buttons that come with this form are set up to create a new record, edit a record, and delete a record.

- Media form, which displays a single record with placeholders for media objects such as images or videos.

- Message box (MsgBox) form, which is used to display messages to users of a database. This form comes with Yes, No, and Cancel buttons. You can use this form to notify users of an impending action and have users indicate whether the action should proceed.

- Tabs form, which presents a form on which you define tabs (or pages) to present and manage a set of related data.

When you select a blank form in the Application Parts gallery, Access prepares the form template and then adds an entry for the form to the Navigation pane. (If the Navigation pane is filtered so that forms are not displayed, you need to change the filter to display the form.) To view the form, in the Navigation pane, right-click the entry for the form, and then click Open. This lets you view what the basic form looks like, but the form is not operational at this point.

> **Tip** Application part forms that you add to a database use a control layout so that all the controls move and resize together. For more information about working with a control layout, see the "Working with control layouts in Layout view" topic in section 4.2, "Set form controls."

To start designing the form, right-click the entry, and then choose Layout View or Design View. (The following screenshot shows the Dialog form open in Design view.) To specify a record source for the form (the table or query that contains the records you want to display and work with in the form), display the property sheet by using its command on the Form Design Tools Design tab. On the property sheet's Data tab, open the list for the Record Source property, and then choose a table or query. To add fields to the form, click Add Existing Fields in the Tools group, and then click Show All Tables in the field list. (You can't assign a record source to a form until you define at least one table in the database.)

The Record Source property specifies
the records that a form displays

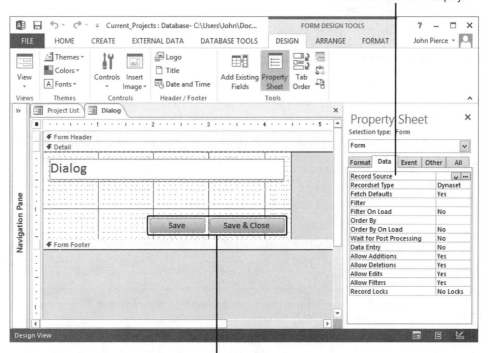

Application part forms include command buttons
programmed to perform specific actions

> **See Also** For more information about defining a record source for a form and adding fields, see section 4.2, "Set form controls."

> **Tip** When you click the ellipsis (...) beside the Record Source in the property sheet, you start the Query Builder. For more information about building queries, see section 3.1, "Create a query."

➤ **To insert a blank form as an application part**

1. On the **Create** tab, in the **Templates** group, click **Application Parts**.

2. In the **Application Parts** gallery, click the type of form you want to add.

3. To view the basic form, in the Navigation pane, double-click the entry for the form.

4. To rename the form, in the Navigation pane, right-click the entry for the form, click **Rename**, and then enter a name for the form.

5. To add controls, fields, and formatting to the form, in the Navigation pane, right-click the form's entry, and then click **Design View** or **Layout View**.

Using Quick Start elements

The Quick Start group in the Application Parts gallery provides a Comments table and four compound application parts for managing contacts, issues, tasks, and users. You can apply these application parts to many types of databases. The ScreenTip that Access displays when you point to an item in this group identifies the objects that the application part contains. (For example, the Issues application part inserts a table named Issues and two forms.)

When you add a Quick Start application part to a database that already includes tables, Access might display the Create Relationship wizard. (Access displays the wizard when it detects that the application part you're adding includes a table that is probably related to one or more existing tables.)

> **See Also** For more information about table relationships and their purpose in an Access database, see section 1.2, "Manage relationships and keys."

The first page in the wizard displays two options for creating a relationship and an option that specifies that there is no relationship. (If you click the There Is No Relationship option, you can still set up a relationship later.)

The first option places the table you're adding on the "many" side of a one-to-many re-lationship. The second option places that table on the "one" side of the relationship. A *one-to-many relationship* occurs when a record in one table is related to many records in another table. The classic example is the relationship between customers and orders. Each customer record in a database is unique (the *one* side of the relationship), but each customer record is related to all the orders placed by the customer (the *many* side of the relationship). Another example is adding the Issues application part to a project or task management database. In this case, each record in the Tasks or Projects table could be related to one or more (many) records in the Issues table.

Click the option for the relationship you want to create. On the next page of the wizard, you specify the field from the table on the "one" side of the relationship that Access will use to create a relationship with the records from the table on the "many" side. In an example involving issues and tasks, you could select a field such as TaskID or TaskTitle to add to the Issues table so that you could associate each issue with a task. Access adds the field you specify to the table on the many side of the relationship, creating a lookup column in that table. In the What Name Would You Like For Your Lookup Column box, enter a name for that column. When you click Create in the wizard, Access adds the table and other objects defined by the application part.

➤ **To insert a Quick Start element as an application part**

1. On the **Create** tab, in the **Templates** group, click **Application Parts**.

2. In the **Application Parts** gallery, click the **Quick Start** application part you want to add.

3. If prompted by Access, complete the **Create Relationship** wizard to set up a rela-tionship between the table being added by the application part and a table already defined in the database.

4. Right-click the entries for any forms added by the application part, click **Rename**, and then enter a name for the form.

5. Right-click the table added by the application part, click **Design View**, and then re-view the fields and properties defined in the table.

6. To add controls, fields, and formatting to a form, right-click the form's entry in the Navigation pane, and then click **Design View** or **Layout View**.

Using earlier Access file formats

When you create a desktop database—either a blank database or a database based on one of the default Access templates—the file uses the .accdb file format. This format is compatible with Access 2007, Access 2010, and Access 2013, but it can't be read by earlier versions of Access.

If members of your organization, department, or workgroup use an earlier version of Access—Access 2000, Access 2002, or Access 2003—you can change the file format in which Access creates new databases by default. By changing the default format to the Access 2000 format or the Access 2002-2003 format (these formats use the file name extension .mdb), you can more easily share the files with those members. You control the file format by adjusting a setting in the Creating Databases area on the General page in the Access Options dialog box.

> **Tip** You can also convert a database by saving it in a format that is compatible with earlier versions of Access. For more information, see the "Using the Save Database As options" topic in section 1.5, "Print and export databases."

➤ **To change the default file format**

1. Click the **File** tab, and then click **Options**.

2. In the **Access Options** dialog box, click **General**.

3. In the **Creating databases** area, in the **Default file format for Blank Database** box, select the file format you want as the default, and then click **OK**.

Practice tasks

The practice file for these tasks is located in the MOSAccess2013\Objective1 practice file folder. You can save the results of the tasks in the same folder.

- Start Access and create a database by using the Desktop Contacts template. (You can view the videos that come with this template to explore it and other features in Access.)

- Open the New page, and use the Custom web app thumbnail to create an Access web app. (Note that you must have access to a SharePoint site that has Access Services enabled, and you must have Full permissions to this site to complete this task.)

- Use the search box on the New page to locate the *Northwind* database, and then save this database to the practice file folder.

- Open the *Marketing_1* database from the practice file folder. Add a Dialog form and a Details form by using application parts.

- Add the Tasks application part to the *Marketing_1* database. In the Create Relationship wizard, click There Is No Relationship.

- Open the Access Options dialog box. On the General tab, explore the options in the Creating databases area. Review other Access options, including those on the Current Databases tab, where you can name your Access application, specify a display form, and select the option Compact On Close.

1.2 Manage relationships and keys

This section describes the role of table relationships, primary keys, and foreign keys in an Access database. First, you study the purpose of defining a primary key for a table and how you set up the primary key. The sections that follow cover the different types of relationships, how to create relationships, and how to edit them.

Specifying primary keys

A table's *primary key* uniquely identifies each record in the table. You can use a single field (for example, a unique product or customer code, or an ID field that is set to the AutoNumber data type that Access provides) or a combination of fields as a table's primary key. A multifield primary key is called a *composite key*. For an AutoNumber field, Access assigns a unique number to each record in a table, so you don't need to keep track of values that might be duplicates. If you don't use the AutoNumber data type but instead use a field whose value you enter, be sure that you set the field's Required property to Yes and that you use a field or a combination of fields whose values change infrequently or not at all.

> **See Also** For information about setting field properties, see section 2.4, "Create and modify fields."

> **Tip** When you create a new table by clicking Table on the Create tab, Access includes an ID field in the table and sets this field to be the table's primary key.

In Access, *key fields* are used when you establish table relationships. For example, if you have a table named *ProjectManagers* whose primary key is the ProjectManagerID field, you can add the ProjectManagerID field to the Projects table to create a relationship between the tables that lets you identify the manager for each project. In the Projects table, the ProjectManagerID field is referred to as a *foreign key*. Primary keys and foreign keys can also be used in queries to join tables; Access uses that relationship to retrieve the set of records that match the criteria you define.

To set the primary key for a table, you must first open the table in Design view. (Select the table in the Navigation pane and then, on the Home tab, on the View menu, click Design View, or simply right-click the table in the Navigation pane and then click Design View.) Click the row selector for the field or fields you want to designate as the primary key (press the Ctrl key and click to select multiple fields), and then click Primary Key in the Tools group on the Table Tools Design tool tab. Access adds a small key icon to the row selector area to indicate that a field is a primary key field.

If you need to remove the primary key designation from a field, open the table in Design view, select the field, and then click Primary Key in the Tools group. To change a table's primary key, remove the current primary key, and then specify the field or fields you want to use.

If a table already contains data, the field or fields you designate for the primary key must have unique values. Also, if a primary key is part of any table relationship, you must remove the relationship before you can change the primary key.

> **See Also** For information about adding and deleting relationships, see the "Setting and viewing relationships" topic later in this section.

➤ **To set a primary key**

1. In the Navigation pane, right-click the table, and then click **Design View**.

2. Select the field or fields you want to designate as the table's primary key. To select multiple fields, press **Ctrl** and select the fields.

3. On the **Table Tools Design** tool tab, click **Primary Key**.

➤ **To remove the primary key designation from a field**

1. In the Navigation pane, right-click the table, and then click **Design View**.

2. Select the field or fields from which you want to remove the primary key designation.

3. On the **Design** tool tab, click **Primary Key**.

Setting and viewing relationships

Formally, Access is known as a *relational database management system*, or RDBMS. In this model, relationships between tables are used to maintain the integrity of the data and to reduce the need to store redundant data. For example, customer names are stored in one table, and orders are stored in another. By creating a relationship between these tables, you don't need to repeat the customer's name in the record for new orders. Table relationships are also used to join tables in queries and to define the record sources for forms and reports.

You define a different type of relationship depending on the data that each table contains.

- **One-to-many relationship** In this relationship, any one record in the first table can be related to many records in the second table (for example, one customer can place many orders), but any record in the second table is related to only one record in the first table (for example, each order is placed by a single customer).

- **One-to-one relationship** In a one-to-one relationship, each record in the first table is related to only one record in the second table. You can use this type of relationship when you want to use a separate table to define and store fields for data that you don't refer to regularly or that you want to keep more confidential. For example, in an Employees table, you can store general employee information such as first and last name, department, job title, and building and office location. In a separate EmployeesRating or EmployeeCompensation table, you can store performance ratings and compensation data—information that you want only certain people or groups to use. Each record in the Employees table has a single matching record in the table for ratings or compensation.

- **Many-to-many relationship** Some tables have a many-to-many relationship. For example, an orders table and a products table have a many-to-many relationship. Each record in the orders table can have many matching records in the products table, and each record in the products table can have many matching order records. You can't define this type of relationship directly. Instead, you need to create a linking table (also known as a junction table) to create two one-to-many relationships. The linking table includes the primary key fields from both the other tables. In the Northwind sample database that comes with Access, the Order Details table is a linking table.

To view and define relationships between tables, click the Database Tools tab, and then click Relationships. Access displays the Relationships window and the Relationship Tools Design tool tab.

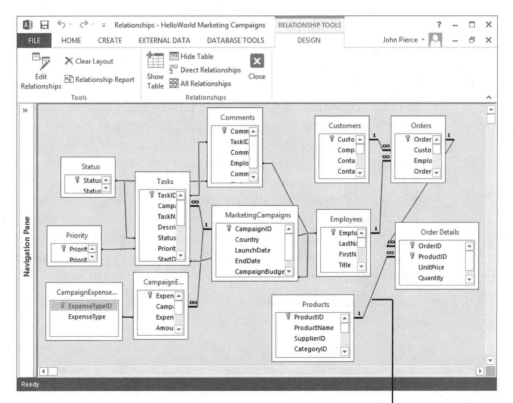

The symbols at the end of this relationship line indicate that this relationship enforces referential integrity

To create a relationship, drag the linking field in the first table (the *one* table in a one-to-many relationship) to the second table (the *many* table). Access then displays the Edit

Relationships dialog box. In the dialog box, if Access detects matching fields, the fields are selected in the Table/Query and Related Table/Query lists. If you need to select a different field in the Related Table/Query list, select that field and then click Create New to establish the relationship. The relationship type is indicated at the bottom of the dialog box.

The Edit Relationships dialog box includes several important options.

- **Enforce Referential Integrity** Referential integrity is used to prevent orphan records (records in one table with no matching record in a related table) and to maintain references between related tables. By using referential integrity, you ensure that no record in one table refers to a record in another table that doesn't exist—for example, a record for a book cannot refer to an author if a record for that author does not exist. If you enforce referential integrity, Access does not allow operations that violate referential integrity rules for that relationship. For example, you can't enter a customer ID in the Orders table if that customer ID does not exist in the Customers table. Also, you can't delete records that remove a target. For example, you can't delete a customer record if order records for that customer exist.

- **Cascade options** If you select Enforce Referential Integrity, you can choose one or both of the Cascade options:

  - Select Cascade Update Related Fields to have Access update the foreign key for all related fields when you make a change to the primary record.

  - Select Cascade Delete Related Records to have Access delete all related records when you delete a primary record. (If you delete a customer, Access would also delete all order records for that customer.)

To modify a relationship in the Relationships window, right-click the line between the tables, and then click Edit Relationship. (Or select the line and then click Edit Relationships on the Design tool tab.) To delete a relationship, right-click the relationship line and click Delete.

> **Tip** To reproduce the layout in the Relationship window in a format you can print, click Relationship Report in the Tools group.

Use the commands in the Relationships group to manage your view of the Relationships window. Select a table, and then click Hide Table to remove it from the window. Click Show Table to display a dialog box in which you can select one or more tables to add to the tables already shown.

To view the relationships for a particular table, click Clear Layout to remove all the tables from the Relationships window, click Show Table, and then select the table whose relationships you want to examine. Click Direct Relationships to display the tables directly related to the table you selected.

When you close the Relationships window, Access prompts you to save the current layout. Click Yes or No depending on your preference.

➤ **To create a table relationship**

1. On the **Database Tools** tab, click **Relationships**.

2. If the tables you need aren't displayed, click **Show Table** in the **Relationships** group (on the **Relationship Tools Design** tool tab), select the tables in the **Show Table** dialog box, and then click **Add**.

3. Drag the linking field in the first table (the "one" table in a one-to-many relationship) to the second table (the "many" table). Access displays the **Edit Relationships** dialog box.

4. In the dialog box, be sure the linking fields are selected in the **Table/Query** and **Related Table/Query** lists.

5. In the **Edit Relationships** dialog box, select **Enforce Referential Integrity** if you want to enable this feature for this relationship. If you enable referential integrity, select one or both of the **Cascade** options.

6. Click **Create** to establish the relationship and close the dialog box.

➤ **To modify a relationship**

1. On the **Database Tools** tab, click **Relationships**.

2. In the **Relationships** window, right-click the relationship line between two tables, and then click **Edit Relationship**.

3. In the **Edit Relationships** dialog box, make changes to the relationship (for example, select **Enforce Referential Integrity** if that option is not yet selected), and then click **OK**.

Practice tasks

The practice file for these tasks is located in the MOSAccess2013\Objective1 practice file folder. You can save the results of the tasks in the same folder.

- Open the *Marketing_1* database from the practice file folder. In the Navigation pane, right-click the *Status* table, and then click Design View. Set the *StatusID* field as the table's primary key.

- With the *Marketing_1* database still open, display the Relationships window, and then add the *Tasks* and *Status* tables to the tables displayed. If you did not create the *Tasks* table in the practice tasks in section 1.1, use the *Tasks_2* table.

- Create a relationship between the *Status* table (*StatusID* field) and the *Tasks* table (*Status* field).

- Use the Show Table command to add the *Compensation* table to the Relationships window. Edit the relationship between the *Compensation* table and the *Employees* table to enforce referential integrity.

- In the Navigation pane, double-click the *RelationshipDemo* form. Use this form to view the sets of records returned by different types of relationships. Right-click the datasheets displayed, and then click Design View to view the relationships.

1.3 Navigate through databases

The navigational tools in an Access database include those common to Office programs and tools that belong only to Access.

As in other Office applications, you use the ribbon to gain access to groups of commands. In Access, these commands are related to inserting, sorting, filtering, and formatting data (all on the Home tab); object creation and related tasks (the Create tab); working with external data (in the Import & Link and Export groups on the External Data tab); and database analysis and maintenance (on the Database Tools tab). In addition, Access provides tool tabs for designing and formatting forms, reports, and other database objects. You can see examples of how to work with the main tabs and many tool tabs in this chapter and the rest of the chapters in this book.

> **Tip** Use the Customize Ribbon entry in the Access Options dialog box to arrange commands on the built-in tabs and create tabs and groups of your own. Use the Quick Access Toolbar option in the Access Options dialog box to add or remove commands from the Quick Access Toolbar.

In an Access database, navigational features can be different for users who are responsible for designing and maintaining the database and for users whose exclusive role is to enter, edit, and view data. Later in this section, you examine how to create a navigation form that greets database users when they open a database and provides a set of controls for opening forms, running queries, and viewing and printing reports. First, you study basic Access views, how to find specific records, and how to set up different views in the Navigation pane.

Working with Access views

You work with database objects in a variety of views. In later chapters, you study examples of how to work with forms and reports in Design view and Layout view. In Design view and Layout view, you can add command buttons, list boxes, and other controls to a form. For reports, you can use these views to apply formatting, group records, add calculated fields, and complete other tasks.

When you define fields and properties for a table, you generally work in table Design view. When you open a table for data entry, you work with the table in Datasheet view. To work with an object in a specific view, open the object from the Navigation pane, and then use the View command on the Home tab (this command also appears on the Design tool tab for objects) to select the view you need. You can also right-click an object in the Navigation pane and then click a view.

Finding records

You have a choice of tools when you need to find a specific record in a table or in the results of a query, or when you're working with a form or report. Use the navigation buttons that appear at the bottom of a form or a table in Datasheet view to move from record to record or to the first or last record. The record indicator displays which record is selected. The navigation area also includes a simple search box. Just enter the text you want to search for. Access finds the first instance of that text in any of the object's fields.

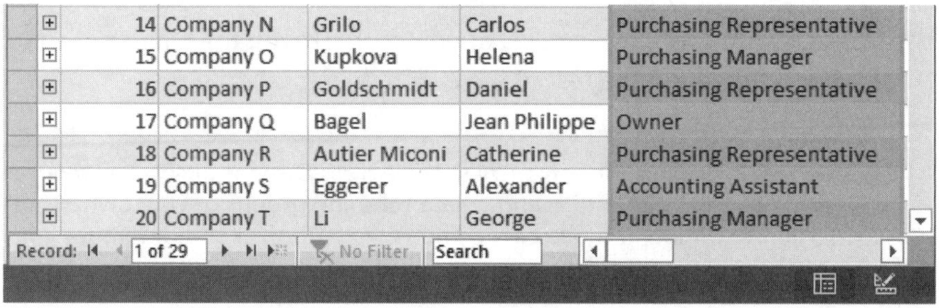
14 Company N Grilo Carlos Purchasing Representative
15 Company O Kupkova Helena Purchasing Manager
16 Company P Goldschmidt Daniel Purchasing Representative
17 Company Q Bagel Jean Philippe Owner
18 Company R Autier Miconi Catherine Purchasing Representative
19 Company S Eggerer Alexander Accounting Assistant
20 Company T Li George Purchasing Manager
Record: 1 of 29
No Filter
Search

On the Home tab, use the commands in the Find group to locate records, perform find-and-replace operations, and move between records by using the Go To options.

Another approach for finding a specific record is to use the options that Access provides for sorting and filtering records. You can sort the records in text fields in ascending or descending order, and in number fields from smallest to largest. To sort and filter records, use the related commands in the Sort & Filter group. You can also right-click a column name in Datasheet view and then click Ascending or Descending, or click the arrow to the right of a column heading to display a menu with sorting and filtering options.

When you filter records, only the records that match the filter's criteria are displayed. This lets you whittle down a long list of records to find just a few records among many.

> **See Also** For information about sorting and filtering records, see the "Finding, sorting, and filtering data" topic in section 2.3, "Manage records."

➤ To navigate between records

1. In the navigation area at the bottom of a table, query, or form, use the arrows to move to the first, next, previous, or last record in the record set.
2. To find a specific record, in the navigation area's search box, enter text related to the record.

➤ To find records

1. On the **Home** tab, in the **Find** group, click **Find**.
2. In the **Find And Replace** dialog box, in the **Find What** box, enter text related to the record you want to locate.
3. Use the **Look In**, **Match**, and **Search** lists and the **Match Case** option to specify conditions that Access will use to locate records.
4. Click **Find Next**.

Configuring the Navigation pane

This section focuses on the Access Navigation pane and how you can modify and organize it to present different views of the objects in a database. The ability to modify the Navigation pane means that it can serve the needs of a range of users—from a database's designer to its casual users.

In some database templates, the Navigation pane is hidden when you first open the database. The Navigation pane is labeled, however, and to expand it, you simply click the arrow at its top. (Click the arrow again to hide the Navigation pane.)

The Northwind sample database provides examples of how you can configure the Navigation pane. In the Northwind database, objects by default are arranged within several categories, not by object name or object type. Objects are grouped under headings such as Customers & Orders, Suppliers, and Shippers instead of headings such as Tables, Queries, and Forms. Headings such as Customers & Orders help clarify functional areas of the database and help users find forms and queries related to the area they are working with.

When you click the arrow (just to the left of the expand/collapse arrow), you display a menu with options for changing how database objects are displayed in the Navigation pane. This menu includes commands in two areas, marked by the shaded labels Navigate To Category and Filter By Group. In the Navigate To Category area, click a built-in category (Object Type, Tables And Related Views, Created Date, and Modified Date). For each category, the Filter By Group area provides options that you can apply to display a subset of objects. For example, if you select Modified Date in the Navigate To Category area, you can then select options such as Today, Three Weeks Ago, Yesterday, Older, or All Dates in the Filter By Group area. For the Object Type category, you can view all objects or only objects of a specific type.

The Tables And Related Views category displays each table in the database together with other database objects that depend on it. Using this view is helpful when you make changes to a table's design. For example, by choosing the Tables And Related Views category and then choosing a single table in the Filter By Group area, you can see which objects depend on the table, and you can review the design of those objects to be sure that the changes you want to make to the table won't affect the other objects in ways you don't intend.

If you right-click the title bar in the Navigation pane, you display a menu with a list of categories (the same categories that are listed in the Navigate To Category area), sorting arrangements (such as Type, Created Date, or Modified Date) and sorting order, and view options. The view options are Details, Icon, and List. The Details view shows each object's name and type and its created and last modified dates. The List view shows names and an identifying icon. The Icon view uses larger icons to identify each object type.

Use the Search bar at the top of the Navigation pane to locate a particular object (or group of objects) by name. As you enter a text string, Access filters the list of objects and displays those that match. Click Clear Search String at the right side of the Search bar to return the Navigation pane to its full view. Right-click the Navigation pane's title bar, and then click Search Bar to show and hide the Search bar.

As with the Northwind sample database, database templates often provide a specific category for viewing database objects by functional role. For example, the Desktop Project Management template provides a category called *Projects Navigation*, which lets you filter by groups such as Projects, Tasks, and Employees. A blank desktop database includes a category named Custom that you can rename and use to build your own Navigation pane view.

To set up Navigation pane categories and groups of your own, right-click the Navigation pane's title bar and click Navigation Options to open the Navigation Options dialog box. (You can open the same dialog box from the Current Database page of the Access Options dialog box.)

The categories defined for the database appear in the list at the left, and each group defined for a category appears in the list at the right. If you want to hide a group from being displayed in the Navigation pane, clear the check box for that group. Use the check boxes in the Display Options area of the dialog box to indicate whether you want to show hidden and system objects in the Navigation pane and to show or hide the Search bar. By using the Open Objects With options, you can control whether an object opens when it is clicked (similar to a hyperlink) or double-clicked in the Navigation pane.

In a new blank database, to modify the built-in Custom category, select it in the Categories list, click Rename Item, and then enter a name for the category. To create and name an additional category, click Add Item, and then click Rename Item to give the category a meaningful name.

In the Groups For list is a group named *Unassigned Objects*, which is a built-in group that contains all the objects in a database. When you work with the default Custom category in a blank database, Access also provides a group named Custom Group 1.

> **Tip** You can reposition a custom category or group by using the arrows that appear beside an item's name. You cannot place a custom category above the two built-in categories or place a custom group below the built-in group Unassigned Objects.

Use the Add Group, Delete Group, and Rename Group buttons to create and modify the groups you want to include in a category. When you finish defining categories and groups, click OK in the Navigation Options dialog box.

You use the Navigation pane to add database objects to a group in a custom category. First, click the category in the Navigate To Category area of the Navigation pane menu. Expand the Unassigned Objects list if it is collapsed, right-click an object you want to add to a new group (use the Ctrl key to select more than one object), click Add To Group, and then click the group you want to add the object or objects to. (You can also drag an object from the Unassigned Objects group to the group where you want to place it.)

When you add a database object to a custom group, you add only a shortcut to that object, not the object itself. This means that you can delete a shortcut from a custom group without deleting the database object. When you right-click an object in a custom group, you can use the Rename Shortcut command to assign a different name to the shortcut. Use the Hide In This Group command to hide the object, and use the Remove command to remove the object from the group. After you have assigned all the unassigned objects to a Navigation pane group, you can return to the Navigation Options dialog box and clear the check box for Unassigned Objects to hide it. You can also right-click the Unassigned Objects heading in the Navigation pane and then click Hide.

➤ **To create and modify Navigation pane categories and groups**

1. Right-click the Navigation pane's title bar, and then click **Navigation Options.**

2. In the **Navigation Options** dialog box, click **Add Item** to add a category.

3. Enter a name for the category.

4. To add a group to the new category, click **Add Group**, and then enter a name for the group.

5. Click **Delete Item** or **Rename Item** to manage categories, and then click **Delete Group** or **Rename Group** to work with custom groups.

6. In the **Display Options** area, select or clear the options for showing hidden objects, system objects, and the Search bar.

7. In the **Open Objects With** area, click **Single-Click** or **Double-Click.**

➤ **To add objects to a group**

1. In the Navigation pane, display the **Unassigned Objects** group or another existing group.

2. Right-click the object you want to add to the group, click **Add to group**, and then select the group.

Building navigation forms

To augment (or replace) the Access Navigation pane, you can build a form that lets database users open forms, run queries, view reports, and perform other database operations without using the Navigation pane.

To start, select one of the layout options from the menu that appears when you click Navigation in the Form group on the Create tab. Each of the built-in layouts provides tabs (in various locations and orientations) that you click to display the object you want to use.

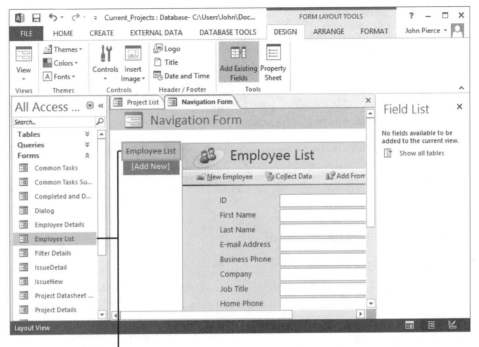

Drag objects from the
Navigation pane to the Add
New area to build a
navigation form

You add forms and reports to the navigation form by dragging them from the Navigation pane to the Add New area in the navigation form.

After you create a navigation form, you can select it as the default form that Access displays when you open the database. Open the Access Options dialog box by clicking Options on the File tab. On the Current Database page, in the Application Options section, select the navigation form in the Display Form list. You can use this option to designate any form in your database as the default form to display. You don't need to select a navigation form.

➤ **To create a navigation form**

1. On the **Create** tab, in the **Forms** group, click **Navigation**, and then click the layout you want to use.

2. Display the Navigation pane if it is not already displayed.

3. In the Navigation pane, select a form or report, and then drag the object to the **Add New** area in the navigation form.

4. Use the **Controls** group on the **Form Layout Tools Design** tab to add other controls to the body of the form.

5. Click **Add Existing Fields** on the **Design** tool tab to open the field list, and then add fields to the form.

➤ **To specify a startup form**

1. Click the **File** tab, and then click **Options**.

2. In the **Access Options** dialog box, on the **Current Database** page, select the form you want to use from the **Display Form** list.

Practice tasks

The practice file for these tasks is located in the MOSAccess2013\Objective1 practice file folder. You can save the results of the tasks in the same folder.

- Open the *Marketing_1* database from the practice file folder.

- Open the *Customers* table. Work with the controls in the record navigation area. Use the search box to locate the record for *The Big Cheese*.

- Create a Navigation pane view named *Campaigns*, and groups named *Campaign Details*, *Products*, and *Employees*. Add tables to these groups to organize the Navigation pane.

- Create a navigation form by using the Vertical Tabs, Left layout. Add the *Task-Details* form to the navigation form. Save the form (use the default name for this practice task), and then set the form as the display form in the Access Options dialog box.

1.4 Protect and maintain databases

In the Backstage view, the Info page provides options for maintaining and protecting a database. The first of these options—Compact & Repair—can help improve the performance of a database and can repair database files in the event of a problem. Use the Encrypt With Password option to restrict database access to only those users who know the password.

This section describes these options in addition to other tasks related to protecting and maintaining a database: working with backups, merging databases, and splitting a database—a step that applies especially to a database shared by multiple users.

Compacting and repairing databases

As you and other users work with an Access database, the file grows larger. Database files can also become corrupt.

A database file grows larger as you add data and because Access creates and uses hidden objects to perform its work behind the scenes. Although an Access file doesn't always become corrupt, frequent use—especially by multiple users working on the database over a network—can result in a corrupted file, which can in some cases result in data loss or affect the ease with which you can change the database's design.

To keep ahead of these potential problems, you can run the Compact & Repair command from the Info page. You might run this command as part of your regular backup routine, for example.

Some restrictions apply to running Compact & Repair. For example, if more than one person has the database open when you run Compact & Repair, Access displays a message indicating that you attempted to open a database that is already open. Before you compact a multiuser database, you should be sure that no one has the database open and then use the Open dialog box to open the database for exclusive access.

> **Tip** Select the Compact On Close option on the Current Database page of the Access Options dialog box to compact a database each time you close it.

If you want to compact a database other than the one that is currently open, close the current database and then click Compact And Repair Database on the Database Tools tab. In the Database To Compact From dialog box, select the database and then click Compact. Access now displays the Compact Database Into dialog box and displays a temporary name for the compacted database in the File Name box. You can use the original name or enter a new name. If you use the original name, Access prompts you to replace the original database. Click Yes in this message box to complete the operation.

➤ **To compact and repair the current database**

1. If you have the database open in read-only mode, click **File**, **Open**, and then use the **Open** dialog box to open the database by using the **Open Exclusive** option. If more than one person has the database open, ask each user to close the database, and then use the **Open** dialog box to open the database by using the **Open Exclusive** option.

2. Click the **File** tab, and then click **Info**.

3. Click **Compact & Repair Database**.

➤ **To compact and repair a database that isn't currently open**

1. Close any open databases.

2. On the **Database Tools** tab, in the **Tools** group, click **Compact and Repair Database**.

3. In the **Database to Compact From** dialog box, select the database you want to compact, and then click **Compact**.

4. In the **Compact Database Into** dialog box, enter a name for the compacted database, and then click **Save**.

5. If you used the current name of the database, click **Yes** in the message box Access displays to confirm that Access should replace the current database file.

Encrypting database files

When you define a password for a database, any user who wants to work with the database must provide the password. You can use this process to restrict who can open a database that is stored in a location that many users share.

A database must be open for exclusive use before you can encrypt the database by using a password. If you are encrypting the current database, you need to close it before you open it for exclusive use.

On the Info tab, click Encrypt With Password. In the Set Database Password dialog box, enter a password and then enter it again to verify it.

> **Tip** If any properties of the database are incompatible with encryption, Access displays a message box telling you that the feature (such as row-level locking) will be ignored. You can safely dismiss this message and proceed with encryption.

To remove a password from a database, first open it for exclusive use. (You need to provide the password to complete this step.) Use the Decrypt Database command on the Info page to remove the password from the database.

➤ To encrypt a database with a password

1. On the **File** tab, click **Open**.
2. Select the location where the database is stored. In the **Open** dialog box, select the database file, click the arrow beside the **Open** button, and then click **Open Exclusive**.
3. Click the **File** tab, click **Info**, and then click **Encrypt with Password**.
4. In the **Set Database Password** dialog box, enter the password you want to use, enter the password again in the **Verify** box, and then click **OK**.

➤ To remove a database password

1. On the **File** tab, click **Open**.
2. Select the location where the database is stored. In the **Open** dialog box, select the database file, click the arrow beside the **Open** button, and then click **Open Exclusive**.
3. Enter the password for the database.
4. Click the **File** tab, click **Info**, and then click **Decrypt Database**.
5. In the **Unset Database Password** dialog box, enter the password applied to the database, and then click **OK**.

Backing up databases

Another step in protecting your data and database files from potential loss and corruption is to perform regular backups. In practice, you need to back up some databases more often than others. A database that serves as an archive, for example, and isn't used frequently, doesn't need to be backed up on a specific schedule. A database that you and others work with nearly every day should be backed up on a regular schedule. You should also follow standard backup procedures such as keeping the backup copies on external media (such as a CD-ROM or a flash drive) and in a secure location.

The Back Up Database command is on the Save As page in the Backstage view, in the list of commands in the Advanced area. When you back up a database, Access appends the current date to the name of the database file. You can retain this date or replace it with an alternative identifier. You might also add "backup" to the file name.

➤ **To back up a database**

1. Click the **File** tab, and then click **Save As**.

2. In the **Advanced** list, click **Back Up Database**, and then click **Save As**.

3. In the **Save As** dialog box, modify the file name that Access provides (or accept the default name), and then click **Save**.

Restoring data from a backup

If one or more objects in a database become corrupt, if you lose data, or if you need to return to an earlier version of a database for some other reason, you can restore a database by replacing it with a backup file. You can also restore specific database objects by importing them from a recent backup.

> **Important** You might be able to at least partially repair a corrupt database by running the Compact & Repair command. For information, see the "Compacting and repairing a database" topic earlier in this section.

To restore a full database file, you can use File Explorer to locate the backup file you want to use and then replace the original file with the backup. To restore specific database objects, you use the Access command in the Import & Link group on the External Data tab.

> **Tip** In Windows 8, File Explorer has replaced Windows Explorer. Throughout this book, we refer to this browsing utility by its Windows 8 name. If your computer is running Windows 7, use Windows Explorer instead.

Restoring an object from a backup doesn't automatically replace the original object. For example, if you import a table named *Tasks* from a recent backup, Access creates a table named *Tasks1* in the current database. Before you begin the steps to restore a database object, delete the object from the current database or rename the original object (by adding an identifier such as "old" or "bad").

You select the objects you want to import by using the Import Objects dialog box. Use the tabs to display database objects of a specific type. (Selecting import options is described in more detail in the "Merging Access databases" topic later in this section.)

➤ **To restore a database object from a backup**

1. Open the database in which to restore an object.

2. Using the Navigation pane, rename or delete the current instance of the object. (If you are restoring a missing object, you can ignore this step.)

3. On the **External Data** tab, click **Access** in the **Import & Link** group.

4. In the **Get External Data** dialog box, click **Import tables, queries, forms, reports, macros, and modules into the current database**.

5. Click **Browse** to locate the backup file you want to use, and then click **OK**.

6. In the **Import Objects** dialog box, select the object or objects you want to restore, and then click **OK**.

7. In the **Get External Data** dialog box, click **Close**.

Merging Access databases

A situation might occur in which you want to modify or extend a database by including one or more database objects from a different database. To accomplish this task, you use the Access command in the Import & Link group on the External Data tab.

You need to open the destination database (the database into which you want to merge objects) and know the location of the database that contains the objects you want to import. After you point Access to the source database, Access displays the Import Objects dialog box. If you don't see the import option controls at the bottom of the dialog box, click Options.

Use these options to control which features are merged. Some options are related to features in earlier versions of Access.

On the Tables, Queries, and other tabs, select the objects you want to import and merge. You need to make selections on each tab. The Select All and Deselect All buttons operate on objects on a single tab, not on all the objects in the database.

To refine the operation, use the options in the Import, Import Tables, and Import Queries areas. For example, in the Import Tables area, you can choose whether to import only table definitions (a table's fields and properties, for example) or both the definition and the table's data.

➤ **To merge databases**

1. Open the destination database (the database into which you want to merge other objects).

2. On the **External Data** tab, click **Access** in the **Import & Link** group.

3. In the **Get External Data** dialog box, click **Import tables, queries, forms, reports, macros, and modules into the current database**.

4. Click **Browse** to locate the source database, and then click **OK**.

5. In the **Import Objects** dialog box, select the object or objects you want to merge, and then click **OK**.

6. In the **Get External Data** dialog box, click **Close**.

Splitting databases

You can think of an Access database as composed of two parts. The tables, which define and store the raw data, make up one part. The second part consists of the queries, forms, reports, and supporting objects that users interact with to enter, edit, and view data. You can *split* a database to store the tables in one file and the other database files in a second file, essentially creating a database with a front end and a back end. Splitting a database allows the database designers and administrators to create new forms or update reports for the front end without having to interfere with the use of the back-end database while doing so. When the new objects are ready, the administrators can implement the updated front end with relationships and references still in place.

Another reason to split a database is to reduce network traffic when the database is used by more than one person. The back-end database (all the tables) can reside in a shared location, and each person can use a local copy of the front-end database. Remember to back up your database before you split it.

➤ **To split a database**

1. Close all open database objects.

2. On the **Database Tools** tab, in the **Move Data** group, click **Access Database**. If Access displays a security notice that shows the path to the file ACWZTOOL.ACCDE, click **Open** to proceed and open the **Database Splitter** dialog box.

3. In the **Database Splitter** dialog box, read through the information provided, and then click **Split Database**.

4. In the **Create Back-end Database** dialog box, choose a location for the back-end file. By default, Access uses the current database name and adds _be to the end of the file name.

5. Click **Split**, and then click **OK** to close the message box.

Practice tasks

The practice file for these tasks is located in the MOSAccess2013\Objective1 practice file folder. You can save the results of the tasks in the same folder.

- Open the *Northwind* database in the practice file folder. (Use the New page to locate and create this database if you did not do so earlier.) Log on by using any user name.

- Create a password for the database.

- Run the Compact & Repair command.

- Create a backup of the database, and then use this backup as the source for restoring a database object.

- Split the *Northwind* database to create a front-end database and a back-end database.

1.5 Print and export databases

You can use the data you store in Access in several ways. Within Access, you can create reports, for example, and distribute the reports in printed or various electronic formats. You can also export data to formats that are compatible with earlier versions of Access and with other programs, including Excel and Word.

This section first focuses on how to print reports and records and how to export data from Access (you can choose from several formats). It then covers a few other related tasks—saving a database as a template, maintaining a database for backward compatibility, and saving a database to an external location.

Printing in Access

The Print tab in the Backstage view offers three options. The first two, Quick Print and Print, provide limited but useful options under specific conditions.

- **Quick Print** Just as the on-screen text describes, this command sends the selected object to the default printer without further intervention. Use this option if you don't need to set any printer options (such as the number of copies to print, a page range, or options for collating or double-sided printing), and you don't need to preview the printout to check layout, orientation, or other page settings.

- **Print** Click Print to open the Print dialog box. Here, you can choose a printer (a network printer, for example), set specific printer properties, specify a page range, and set the number of copies to print. Click Setup to open the Page Setup dialog box, where you can make changes to the page margins or set an option for printing headings.

➤ **To print a report**

➜ Right-click the report, and then click **Print** to print the full report directly to the default printer.

　Or

1. Open the report from the Navigation pane.
2. Click the **File** tab, click **Print**, and then click **Quick Print** or **Print**.

➤ **To print selected records from a table or a query in Datasheet view**

1. Open the table or query.
2. Select the records, click the **File** tab, and then click **Print**.
3. Click the **Print** option to open the **Print** dialog box. In the **Print range** area, click **Selected Records**. If you don't click **Selected Records**, Access prints all the records in the datasheet.

Working in Print Preview

The third option on the Print tab is Print Preview. Click Print Preview to display the Print Preview tab on the ribbon and gain access to options related to page size, page layout, and zoom levels.

> **Tip** The Print Preview tab also provides a set of options (in the Data group) for exporting data to other programs or in various formats. These options are described in the "Exporting data" topic later in this section.

When you design and format a report in Design view or Layout view, the Page Setup tab (under Report Design Tools or Report Layout Tools) provides many of the commands also available on the Print Preview tab. You can use the Page Setup tab options as you work with the report to define margins and page orientation and to make other settings related to printing the report.

Page Size options

In the Page Size group, click Size to display a menu of standard paper sizes, including letter, legal, and A4. This menu does not provide an option to create a custom page size.

Click Margins to open a menu where you can choose the Normal, Wide, or Narrow option. This menu includes a Custom Margins option if the object's margin settings differ from one of the standard options.

The Show Margins option displays or hides margins, and the Print Data Only option removes elements, such as column headings and information in page headers and footers, from the information that Access prints.

Page Layout options

The Page Layout group contains four options. Click Portrait or Landscape to set the page orientation. Use the Columns command to set up a report (such as a product or contact list) in a specific number of columns.

Click Page Setup to open the Page Setup dialog box. This dialog box duplicates many of the options available through the commands in the Page Size and Page Layout groups and also lets you refine these settings further.

Zoom options

By clicking Zoom, you can choose one of several zoom settings to enlarge or compress the view. The range of zoom levels extends from 10 percent to a maximum of 1000 percent (not all zoom levels apply to every object), but you can choose only preset options (such as 75% or 200%). You can use the Zoom slider, in the lower-right corner of the Access window, to adjust the zoom level with greater flexibility.

The Zoom group also lets you choose how many pages to display in a multipage report or printout. By default, 1 page is displayed. You can also display 2, 4, 8, or 12 pages. The last three of these options appear when you click More Pages.

➤ **To manage an object in Print Preview**

1. Open the database object you want to print.

2. Click **File**, **Print**, and then click **Print Preview**.

3. Use the **Page Size** group to adjust paper size and margins and to specify whether only data should be printed.

4. Use the **Page Layout** group to set the page orientation, columns, and other page setup options.

5. Use the **Zoom** group to zoom in or out.

Exporting data

You can do a lot with the data you enter and maintain in an Access database. You can export data, for example, to use it in other programs and in other contexts. Data related to sales, budgets, orders, and other financial records can be exported to Excel for analysis. A list of contacts can be exported to a list in a SharePoint site or used in a mail merge in Word. Exporting data to a text file or to an XML file makes the data compatible with other database and spreadsheet programs, and creating a PDF or an XPS file by using an export operation lets you distribute data in formats designed for review instead of analysis and editing. Access also provides other export options, all available in the Export group on the External Data tab.

To begin exporting data, open the database object you want to export by using the Navigation pane. In the Export dialog box, you can select options to maintain an object's formatting and layout when you export it, view the exported file when the operation is complete, and export only selected records (in lieu of the complete record set that is contained in a specific table or query, for example). Specific operations, such as exporting to a text file, require you to set additional options that control where and how data is exported. You can also save export settings and then repeat an export operation in a single step.

> **Tip** You can move a database to a SharePoint site by using the SharePoint command in the Move Data group on the Database Tools tab. If Access encounters any issues moving the database objects to SharePoint, Access creates a table named *Move to SharePoint Site Issues*. Open this table to read a description of the issues, such as incompatible data types or invalid URLs.

Exporting to Excel

The default setting for exporting Excel data is the Excel Workbook file format (.xlsx). Access uses the database object's name as the exported file name. (You can click Browse to save the file in a different folder—perhaps in a shared network location—and you can also replace the default file name with one of your own.) In the File Format list, the options depend on the type of object you export. When you export records from a query, for example, you can keep Excel Workbook (.xlsx) or choose Excel Binary Workbook, Microsoft Excel 5.0/95 Workbook, or Excel 97–Excel 2003 Workbook. If you export a report, the file formats are limited to Microsoft Excel 5.0/95 Workbook and Excel 97–Excel 2003 Workbook.

The availability of the export options also depends on the type of object. If you export a report, the Export Data With Formatting And Layout check box is selected by default and cannot be cleared. If you export a query or a table, you can select or clear the formatting and layout check box. By selecting that check box, you can open the destination file, and if you selected a subset of the records, you can then choose to export only those records.

If you export an object's complete record set, Access displays another dialog box, which has an option for saving the export steps. Select this option if you expect to run this export operation again using the same object and the same export settings.

Exporting text files

When you export data to a text file, the steps you follow depend on the whether you select the Export Data With Formatting And Layout check box. When this check box is selected, Access displays the Encode As dialog box. If you don't select Export Data With Formatting And Layout, Access displays the Export Text wizard.

In the Encode As dialog box, choose one the following encoding schemes, depending on where the exported data will be used: Windows (Default), MS-DOS, Unicode, or Unicode (UTF-8). The Windows (Default) and MS-DOS options apply to text files that will be used only in programs that support these formats. Most programs consuming text files can use files encoded with the Unicode option. Unicode (UTF-8) is a format used widely on the web.

In export operations that rely on the Export Text wizard, you first specify whether to export the data as a delimited text file or as a fixed-width text file.

From this point, the wizard displays screens that refine your initial choice. For example, for delimited text files, you specify the character that separates fields in each record (often a comma), whether to include field names in the first row of the exported file, and the text qualifier character (which is used to handle instances of the delimiting character that appear in actual values). For fixed-width exports, you use the wizard to indicate where field breaks occur by dragging lines to create columns.

> **Tip** Use the Advanced button in the Export Text wizard to open a dialog box that you use to create and save an export specification. You can specify an export specification in a VBA module in an automated text export.

Exporting to XML files

When you export data to an XML file, you have the option to also export the schema for the data (an XSD file) and the presentation of the data (which is defined in an XSL file).

Each of these options have additional settings, which you display by clicking More Options in the Export XML dialog box. For the data, you can export records in related tables in addition to the data in the object you selected. You can also specify an encoding scheme (UTF-8) or (UTF-16). Among the options related to exporting the schema are whether to include table and field properties, and whether to embed the schema in the XML file or create a separate schema document. Presentation options include the location where the XLS file is stored, where related images are stored, and whether the XSL transformation is run from a client or a server computer. In the Run From area, the Client option creates an HTML file on the local computer that programmatically merges the XSL file and the data (XML) file. This option does not embed the presentation information in the data, which lets you update either the XSL file or the XML file without having to run the export operation again. The Server (ASP) option creates an Active Server Pages (ASP) file that merges the presentation with the data and sends the HTML file that's created to the local computer.

Saving export steps

At the end of export operations, Access displays the Export dialog box, which contains an option you can select to save the export steps you defined.

Update the name that Access provides in the Save As box and add a description. Use the Create An Outlook Task area to set up a reminder in Outlook that prompts you to run this export operation again when required.

When you want to run a saved export in Access, on the External Data tab, in the Export group, click Saved Exports. Access opens the Manage Data Tasks dialog box. This dialog box provides options to run the export, create an Outlook task, modify the name or description provided earlier, and delete any saved exports (or saved imports) that you no longer need.

➤ **To export data from Access**

1. Open the object that contains the data you want to export.

2. On the **External Data** tab, in the **Export** group, click the format or program you want to export to.

3. In the **Export** dialog box, specify the file name and location, and select the export options you want to use: to include formatting and layout, to view the exported file, and to export only selected records.

4. Depending on the export option you select in step 2, use the dialog boxes and wizards Access provides to specify file format and related export options.

➤ **To save export steps**

1. In the **Export** dialog box, select **Save export steps**.

2. Enter a name for the export steps (or accept the default name) and enter a description.

3. If you want to, select the option **Create Outlook Task**.

4. Click **Save Export**.

➤ **To run a saved export**

1. On the **External Data** tab, in the **Export** group, click **Saved Exports**.

2. In the **Manage Data Tasks** dialog box, select the export operation you want to run, and then click **Run**.

Saving databases as templates

The Save As page in the Backstage view includes an option (in the Database File Types area) that lets you save a database as a template. You might use this option after you create a basic database that includes contact information you need in more than one database, or after you create a set of forms with a look and feel that you want each database to include.

To define a template, you work with the Create New Template From This Database dialog box.

Create New Template from This Database ? ×

Name:

Department Projects

Description:

Use this template for all department project databases

Category:

In House

Icon: Displayed as 64x32 pixels

icon.png

Preview:

preview.png

Primary Table:

Orders

Instantiation Form:

☑ Application Part

☐ Include Data in Template

Learn more about advanced template properties.

Share your template with the community.

OK   Cancel

In the dialog box, provide a name and description for the template. In the Category box, User Templates is shown by default, but you can use a category of your own if you prefer. If you plan to share this template with other users or just want to add a professional touch to a template you're creating for yourself, you can specify image files to use as an icon for the template (this icon replaces the standard Access icon in the program's application window) and as the thumbnail preview of the template that appears in the Backstage view. If you select the Application Part check box, you should specify a primary table that Access uses as the default option in the Create Relationship wizard. Select the Include Data In Template option to keep the data already stored in the database as part of the template.

Use the Instantiation Form list when you want to display a splash screen or a form that performs a startup routine. Access displays the form you select in this list only once and then deletes the form. Be careful not to confuse this option with a startup form, which you can specify for the current database by using the Access Options dialog box.

> **See Also** For more information about application parts, see the "Working with application parts" topic in section 1.1, "Create new databases." For more information about startup forms, see the "Building navigation forms" topic in section 1.3, "Navigate through databases."

By default, templates are stored in your user profile, in \AppData\Roaming\Microsoft\Templates\Access.

If you selected the Application Part option when you saved the template, the template is available in the Application Parts gallery on the Create tab. The application part appears under the heading you provided in the Category box in the Create New Template From This Database dialog box. The template is also available when you click the Personal link on the Access startup screen or on the New page in the Backstage view.

> ➤ **To save a database as a template**

1. Create and format the database objects you want to include in the template. Enter any data you want the template to store by default.

2. Click the **File** tab, and then click **Save As**. In the **Database File Types** list, click **Template**, and then click **Save As**.

3. In the **Create New Template from this Database** dialog box, enter a name and description for the database, and then specify a category, icon image, preview image, and instantiation form (if you want to use one).

4. Select **Application Part** to add this template to the **Application Parts** gallery, and then specify a primary table for the template.

5. Select **Include Data in Template** as applicable.

Using the Save Database As options

Sections earlier in this chapter have addressed a few of the options on the Save As page in the Backstage view: saving a database in a different file format, saving a database as a template, and backing up a database. This section provides more details about working with earlier file formats and covers two options in the Advanced area of the Save As page: Package And Sign, and Make ACCDE. These options are used by database developers and administrators as a means to distribute a database to its users.

Saving files in earlier formats

With Save Database As selected, the options in the Database File Types list are the default format (.accdb) or the format used in Access 2002–2003 or Access 2000. You should select the Access 2002–2003 or Access 2000 format when you need to share a database with users who are working with those versions of the program.

If you select any of the first three options, Access displays the standard Save As dialog box, with the format you selected as the only option available in the Save As Type list. Keep in mind, however, that Access 2013 comes with features that can keep you from saving a database to an earlier file format. For example, the encryption mechanism used with .accdb files is different from the format used in earlier versions of Access. You need to remove a password from an Access 2013 database before you can save it in an earlier file format. A database that includes new data types or property settings cannot be saved in an earlier format. For example, using the Attachment data type or calculated fields in tables prevents you from saving an .accdb file in an earlier file format.

> **See Also** For more information about encrypting and decrypting a database, see the "Encrypting database files" topic in section 1.4, "Protect and maintain databases."

Even though Access 2007 uses the same file format as Access 2013, some features in Access can prevent you from modifying or opening database objects in Access 2007, or from opening the database itself.

> **To save a database file in a different format**

1. Click the **File** tab, click **Save As**, and then click **Save Database As**.
2. In the **Database File Types** list, select the format you want to use, and then click **Save As**.
3. In the **Save As** dialog box, enter a name for the database, open the location where you want to save the file, and then click **Save**.

Packaging and signing databases

If you need to distribute and deploy an Access database to a group of users, you can use the Package And Sign option to create an Access deployment file (.accdc) that includes a digital signature identifying the source of the database. You can place the package in a location where users can retrieve the file. Users extract the database file from the package and then start working with the database. You can apply the Package And Sign option only to databases saved in the newer formats, including .accdb and .accde.

> **Important** Before you can digitally sign a database, you need a digital certificate. You can obtain a digital certificate from a certificate authority such as VeriSign (*www.verisign.com*).

When you select Package And Sign and then click Save As, Access displays a Windows Security dialog box. Select the certificate you want to use to sign the database and then click OK. In the Create Microsoft Access Signed Package dialog box, enter a name for the database package (Access provides a default name by appending the current date to the name of the database), open the location where you want to store the package, and then click Create.

When a user double-clicks the package file to extract the database, Access displays a security notice if the database comes from a source that is not among the user's trusted publishers. A user can view the details of the digital certificate from the dialog box to identify the source of the database. When a user clicks Open in the Microsoft Access Security Notice dialog box, Access displays the Extract Database To dialog box, in which a user specifies where to save the database file.

➤ **To package and sign a database**

1. Click the **File** tab, click **Save As**, and then click **Save Database As**.

2. In the **Advanced** list, select **Package and Sign**, and then click **Save As**.

3. In the **Windows Security** dialog box, select the certificate you want to use to sign the database, and then click **OK**.

4. In the **Create Microsoft Access Signed Package** dialog box, enter a name for the database, open the location where you want to save the file, and then click **Create**.

Creating executable files

When you create an executable file (which uses the .accde file name extension), Access compiles any VBA code the database includes. The operations defined by the code are still available in the database, but users can't view or modify the code. Also, in an .accde database, users can't open forms or reports in Layout or Design view to modify them. Creating an executable file helps maintain a small file size in a database that contains a significant amount of VBA code.

When you choose the Make ACCDE option, Access displays the Save As dialog box. Use this dialog box to specify the file's name and choose a location in which to save it. (Depending on a user's security settings, a Microsoft Access Security Notice dialog box might be displayed when the user opens the .accde file. Click Open in this dialog box to run the database file.)

➤ **To create an executable-only database**

1. Click the **File** tab, click **Save As**, and then click **Save Database As**.

2. In the **Advanced** list, select **Make ACCDE**, and then click **Save As**.

3. In the **Save As** dialog box, enter a name for the database, open the location where you want to save the file, and then click **Save**.

Practice tasks

The practice file for these tasks is located in the MOSAccess2013\Objective1 practice file folder. You can save the results of the tasks in the same folder.

- Open the *Marketing_1* database from the practice file folder.

- Open the *Customers* report from the Navigation pane, and then view the report in print preview. Use the Page Size, Page Layout, and Zoom options to work with the report.

- Export the *Customers* report to Word (to the Rich Text format).

- Export the *Customers* table to Excel and to another Access database.

- Save the *Marketing_1* database as a template. Save the template as an application part in a custom category you create.

Objective review

Before finishing this chapter, be sure you have mastered the following skills:

1.1 Create new databases

1.2 Manage relationships and keys

1.3 Navigate through databases

1.4 Protect and maintain databases

1.5 Print and export databases

2 Build tables

The skills tested in this section of the Microsoft Office Specialist exam for Microsoft Access 2013 relate to building tables. Specifically, the following objectives are associated with this set of skills:

2.1 Create a table

2.2 Format tables

2.3 Manage records

2.4 Create and modify fields

Chapter 1, "Create and manage databases," explained that database templates (desktop templates and templates for Access web apps) provide a set of default tables. This chapter guides you in studying methods for working more with tables, specifically, how to refine their design and enter and update data. This chapter also describes how to create and design tables from scratch. As one of the first steps in creating a database from the ground up—before actually using Access to create tables, forms, and other database objects—you should define which tables you need, how those tables are related, which fields each table requires, and the names of fields. Knowing details such as these makes the process of building tables in Access more efficient.

> **Practice Files** To complete the practice tasks in this chapter, you need the practice files contained in the MOSAccess2013\Objective2 practice file folder. For more information, see "Download the practice files" in this book's Introduction.

2.1 Create a table

You work with tables in two views: Design view and Datasheet view. In Design view, Access doesn't display data. Design view shows only the structure of a table—the fields that make up the table and the settings for properties that define the fields. Datasheet view displays the data in a table, in a grid of columns and rows (resembling the cells in a worksheet in Microsoft Excel). Each column represents a field, and each row represents a record in the table.

This section describes the basics of building tables in Design view and Datasheet view. It also examines Access data types (which you apply to manage the data a field contains), methods for importing data to create a table, and adding a table to an Access web app.

> **See Also** For information about using an application part to insert a table in a database, see the "Working with application parts" topic in section 1.1, "Create new databases."

Defining tables in Design view

With a database open, click the Create tab and then click Table Design to create a table in Design view. In this view, you define fields by working with three main columns: Field Name, Data Type, and Description. The first two columns are required. Adding information to the Description column is optional, but describing important fields in a table is an effective way to start documenting your database.

> **Tip** Adding a concise explanation in the Description column also assists users of the database, because Access displays this description in the status bar when the field is selected in Datasheet view or in a form.

Read the descriptions shown here to learn more about defining a table and about field properties

After entering a name for a field, open the list in the Data Type column. The data type you select defines what sort of data you want to store in the field. The following list describes Access data types:

- **Short Text** Use the Short Text data type for simple text fields. Simple text fields include contact or project names or information such as street addresses or postal codes, which include numbers that aren't used in mathematical operations. By default, Access sets the Field Size property for a Short Text field to 255 characters, which is the maximum number of characters a Short Text field can contain. You can set the Field Size property to a shorter length.

> **Tip** You can set many different properties for the fields in a table. You can set some field properties when working in Datasheet view, including the Name, Caption, Description, Default Value, and Field Size properties. To work with the full range of field properties, you need to open the table in Design view. For more information, see the "Working with field properties" topic in section 2.4, "Create and modify fields."

- **Long Text** The Long Text data type is designed for fields in which you want to store large blocks of text. You can store approximately 1 gigabyte (GB) of alphanumeric data in a Long Text field, but not all that data will be displayed on a form or in a control on a report.

- **Number** Use the Number field to store numeric data of various field sizes, including Byte, Integer, Long Integer, and Decimal. You should choose a field size according to the size and kind of numbers you will store in the field:

    - **Byte** A 1-byte integer containing values from 0 through 255.

    - **Integer** A 2-byte integer containing values from –32,768 through 32,767.

    - **Long Integer** A 4-byte integer containing values from –2,147,483,648 through 2,147,483,647.

    - **Single** A 4-byte, floating-point number containing values from -3.4×1038 through 3.4×1038 and up to seven significant digits.

    - **Double** An 8-byte, floating-point number containing values from $-1.797 \times 10,308$ through $1.797 \times 10,308$ and up to 15 significant digits.

    - **Replication ID** A 16-byte globally unique identifier (GUID).

    - **Decimal** A 12-byte integer with a specified decimal precision that can contain values from approximately -9.999×1027 through 9.999×1027. The default precision (number of decimal places) is 0, and the default scale is 18.

- **Date/Time** Designed to store dates and times. You can choose formats such as Short Date (3/08/2012) and Long Date (Monday, May 23, 2011). You can perform calculations on the data in Date/Time fields to determine the interval between two dates, for example.

- **Currency** Use this data type for monetary values. You can specify formats that include up to four decimal places.

- **AutoNumber** Use AutoNumber for fields for which you want Access to generate a unique identifying number. A table can have only one AutoNumber field that is set to the field size Long Integer. An AutoNumber field is often used as a table's primary key (the field or combination of fields that uniquely identifies each record in a table).

> **See Also** For information about setting a table's primary key, see section 1.2, "Manage relationships and keys."

- **Yes/No** Designed for fields whose value is true or false. In Yes/No fields, Access stores –1 for true (yes) or 0 for false (no).

- **OLE Object** An OLE object field is used to store objects such as pictures or charts created in another Windows–based application. You can store objects up to about 2 GB.

- **Hyperlink** Use the Hyperlink data type for fields in which you want to store a website address (on the Internet or an intranet) or the path to a file (on a network or the local computer).

- **Attachment** By applying the Attachment data type, you create a field in which you can store documents, spreadsheets, presentations, and other file types. You can include an unlimited number of attachments per record, although you are restricted by the limitation on the overall size of an Access database (approximately 2 GB).

- **Calculated** Use the Calculated data type for a field in which you define an expression that uses data from one or more other fields. Calculated fields include a Result Type property that lets you specify the data type for the result of the calculation.

- **Lookup wizard** Use the Lookup wizard entry in the Data Type list to create a field that uses values from a related table or in a list you define. You can create a complex lookup field to store more than one value of the same data type in each record.

> **Tip** Data types for Access web apps are similar to those for desktop databases in the preceding list. Data in a web app is stored in a Microsoft SQL Server database (or a Windows Azure SQL Database for web apps on a Microsoft Office 365 site). For more information about how Access web app data types correspond to SQL Server data types, see the Access help system topic "Data types for Access apps."

You can add a field to a table by using the first blank row, or you can insert a field between fields that are already defined. To insert a field between defined fields, click in the row above where you want to insert the field, and then on the Table Tools Design tool tab, click Insert Rows. (You can also right-click the row and then click Insert Rows.) To delete a field, click in the row, and then click Delete Rows on the Design tool tab (or click Delete Rows on the shortcut menu).

> **Important** If you click Delete Rows for a field that is part of a relationship, Access prevents you from deleting the field.

➤ **To create a table in Design view**

1. On the **Create** tab, click **Table Design**.

2. Use the **Field Name**, **Data Type**, and **Description** columns to define the table's fields.

3. Select the field or fields you want to use as the table's primary key, and then click **Primary Key** on the **Table Tools Design** tool tab.

4. On the **Quick Access Toolbar**, click **Save**.

5. In the **Save As** dialog box, enter a name for the table, and then click **OK**.

> **Tip** If you save a table without defining a primary key, Access displays a message box. Click Yes to have Access create a primary key; click No to save the table without creating a primary key.

Creating tables in Datasheet view

Defining a table in Design view might seem abstract. In Design view, Access displays only the definitions for the data that a table will hold but not the data itself. In contrast, by building a table in Datasheet view, you can begin defining the structure of a table as you compile the data you want to store and manage. Enter field names at the top of a column, and then start entering data for a field. On the basis of the data you enter, Access assigns a data type to that field. (You can also select data types yourself.)

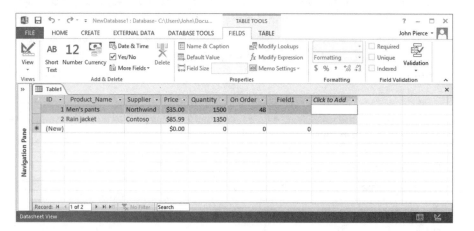

You can use the commands in the Add & Delete group (on the Table Tools Fields tool tab) to create additional fields for the table. Click the command related to the data type you want to use. The Fields tool tab also provides commands for setting a field's format and an array of field properties.

> **See Also** For more information about working with these commands, see section 2.4, "Create and modify fields."

Importing data into a table

One way to build a table is to import data from Excel workbooks, text files, XML files, Microsoft SharePoint lists, and Microsoft Outlook folders. The commands for importing data in these and other formats are in the Import & Link group on the External Data tab.

When you import data, you usually have three options: importing the source data into a new table, appending the data to a table that's already defined, or linking to the data source to create a linked table. (The second and third options are described later in this chapter.)

> **Tip** You can save the settings you use to import data and then run the import operation later by using the saved settings.

Access can use column headings in the source data as field names, and Access often displays a wizard that helps you provide the information Access requires to import data from a particular format.

Importing data from Excel

Click Excel in the Import & Link group to display the Get External Data dialog box, which you use to select an import option and identify the source file. With the Import The Source Data Into A New Table In The Current Database option selected, you use the Import Spreadsheet wizard to complete the operation.

As you work through the wizard, first you either specify the worksheet you want to import or click the Show Named Ranges option and then specify a range. You can scroll through the sample data displayed in the wizard, but you cannot modify it. Select the First Row Contains Column Headings check box if the worksheet you're importing includes column headings that Access can use as field names. You can also specify each field's data type and whether Access should index the field.

Select a field in the preview area by clicking its column heading,
and then specify the settings you want in the Field Options area.
You can also select the option to skip a field.

	Import Spreadsheet Wizard

You can specify information about each of the fields you are importing. Select fields in the area below. You can then modify field
information in the 'Field Options' area.

Field Options

Field Name: ProductName   Data Type: Short Text ▾

Indexed: No ▾   ☐ Do not import field (Skip)

	ProductName	OrderID
1	Queso Cabrales	10248
2	Singaporean Hokkien Fried Mee	10248
3	Mozzarella di Giovanni	10248
4	Manjimup Dried Apples	10249
5	Tofu	10249
6	Manjimup Dried Apples	10250
7	Jack's New England Clam Chowder	10250
8	Louisiana Fiery Hot Pepper Sauce	10250
9	Louisiana Fiery Hot Pepper Sauce	10251
10	Gustaf's Knäckebröd	10251
11	Ravioli Angelo	10251
12	Geitost	10252
13	Sir Rodney's Marmalade	10252
14	Camembert Pierrot	10252

Cancel   < Back   Next >   Finish

The wizard's fourth page shows options for setting the table's primary key. Let Access
create an ID field in the table to use as the primary key, choose your own primary key, or
specify no primary key. When you click Finish in the wizard, Access again displays the Get
External Data dialog box and provides an option for you to save the import steps. Select
this check box if you expect to import this data frequently. Use the text boxes Access
displays to name and describe the import steps. You can also set up a task in Outlook to
remind you to run this import operation again.

> **See Also** For more information about running saved import and export operations, see
> section 1.5, "Print and export databases."

➤ **To import data from Excel into a new table**

1. On the **External Data** tab, in the **Import & Link** group, click **Excel**.

2. In the **Get External Data** dialog box, click the option **Import the source data into a
new table in the current database**, click **Browse** to locate the source file, and then
click **OK**.

3. In the **Import Spreadsheet** wizard, select the worksheet or named range that has the data you want to import.

4. Click **Next** to work through the wizard to specify whether the first column of the data includes column headings, set field options, designate a primary key, and name the table.

5. Click **Finish** in the wizard, and then select the option **Save import steps** in the **Get External Data** dialog box if you want to save the steps in this operation.

Importing data from another Access database

In Chapter 1, "Create and manage databases," you saw two examples of when you use the Access command in the Import & Link group to manage databases—when you want to merge databases and when you want to restore a database object from a backup. You also use this command to import data from another Access database.

In the Get External Data dialog box, locate the database that contains the source data. Choose the first option—Import Tables, Queries, Forms, Reports, Macros, And Modules Into The Current Database. When you click OK, Access displays the Import Objects dialog box, which lists the objects in the source database on separate tabs.

To import data into your database, on the Tables tab, select the items you want to import. Click Options to display the Import, Import Tables, and Import Queries areas of the dialog box.

- **Import** If you are importing more than one related table and want to preserve the tables' relationship, select the Relationships option. Use the Menus And Toolbars option to import any custom menus and toolbars from databases created in versions of Access prior to Access 2007. Use the Import/Export Specs option to include any import or export specifications defined in the source database. Select Nav Pane Groups to import any custom Navigation pane groups set up in the source database, and select All Images And Themes to include these elements with the import.

> **See Also** For more information about using the Import/Export Specs option, see the "Creating an import spec" sidebar later in this section.

- **Import Tables** Use the Definition And Data option to import the data along with the table's structure. Select Definition Only if you want to import only the framework for the table (fields and field and table property settings) but not the data the table contains.

- **Import Queries** Use the options in this area to import a query as a table or as a query.

➤ **To import data from another Access database**

1. On the **External Data** tab, click **Access** in the **Import & Link** group.

2. In the **Get External Data** dialog box, click **Browse** to locate the source database.

3. Click **Import tables, queries, forms, reports, macros, and modules into the current database**, and then click **OK**.

4. In the **Import Objects** dialog box, select the table or tables (or other objects) you want to import. Click **Options** to set options for the import operation.

5. In the **Get External Data** dialog box, select **Save import steps** if you want to save the steps in this operation.

Importing text files

You can import data from a text file that uses the .txt, .csv, .tab, or .asc file name extension. After you select a file and click OK in the Get External Data dialog box, Access displays the Import Text wizard. On the first page, indicate whether a specific character separates (delimits) the fields of data in the text file or whether the data is aligned in fixed-width columns. The option you choose here determines the information you need to provide on the wizard's second page. For delimited text files, you need to specify which character to use as a delimiter. For fixed-width files, you indicate where column breaks should occur.

The remaining pages of the Import Text wizard are like those you work with in the Import Spreadsheet wizard. The wizard lets you rename fields, specify a data type, indicate whether the field should be indexed, and skip a particular field. The wizard also prompts you to set up a primary key for the table.

Creating an import spec

When you click the Advanced button in the Import Text wizard, Access displays the Import Specification dialog box. You can specify settings in this dialog box and save those settings in an import specification file that you can then apply to the text file the next time you import it. Among the settings you specify in this dialog box are file format (delimited or fixed-width), field delimiter, date format information, field names, and data types. Click Save As to save the specification. When you need to use the settings again, click Advanced in the Import Text wizard, click Specs in the Import Specification dialog box, select the specification you need, and then click Open. The settings are applied in the wizard, so you simply need to click Finish to import the text file.

➤ **To import data from a text file into a new table**

1. On the **External Data** tab, click **Text File** in the **Import & Link** group.

2. In the **Get External Data** dialog box, click **Import the source data into a new table in the current database**, click **Browse** to locate the source file, and then click **OK**.

3. In the **Import Text** wizard, specify the format for the file you are importing (**Delimited** or **Fixed Width**), and then click **Next**.

4. Choose the delimiting character or specify column breaks (depending on the format selected in step 3). Select **First Row Contains Field Names** if this option applies.

5. Click **Next**, and then work through the remaining pages to set field options, designate a primary key, and name the table.

6. Click **Finish.** If you want to save the steps in this operation, select **Save import steps** in the **Get External Data** dialog box.

Importing data from other formats

You can also import data from an XML file, a SharePoint list, and other formats. The steps you follow to import data from these formats are essentially the same as for text files or an Excel worksheet. For a SharePoint list, for example, type the address for the SharePoint site in the Get External Data dialog box. Select the option to import the data into a new table. After you click OK, you might need to provide your user name and password to gain access to the SharePoint site. If Access connects to the site successfully, the lists stored on the site are displayed. Use the check boxes to select the list or lists you want to import. If you select more than one list, each list is imported as a separate table.

Importing a contacts or tasks folder from Outlook is an effective way to add this information to a database. Select Outlook Folder in the More list in the Import & Link group. Choose the folder you want to import, and then click Next; Access displays the Import Exchange/Outlook wizard. Use the wizard to provide field names, specify data types, set up indexes, and skip fields. Also choose whether you want Access to generate a primary key. After you name the table and then click Finish, Access displays its standard prompt that lets you save the import steps.

Using linked tables

Linked tables let you refer to and use information that's stored in an external data source. You can create a linked table that's based on an Excel worksheet, a text file, or one of the other external data formats that Access 2013 supports. Linking to an Excel worksheet or a text file, for example, creates a one-way link. You can read the data in Access, but you cannot insert or update records—the data is maintained only in the external data source. However, you can link to tables in another Access database and work with those tables in the same way you work with tables in your database.

> **Tip** You can link to tables in other Access databases to work around the restriction on the size of a single Access database file (approximately 2 GB).

If you link to an Access database or to another external data source that is protected with a password, you need to provide the password to link successfully. Access can save the password so that you don't need to provide it each time you open the external table. Because Access saves this information, you might want to encrypt your database.

> **See Also** For more information, see section 1.4, "Protect and maintain databases."

Linking to a table in another Access database

Use the Access command in the Import & Link group (on the External Data tab) to open the Get External Data dialog box. Click Link To The Data Source By Creating A Linked Table, and then locate the database you want to link to. You use the Link Tables dialog box to select the table or tables you want to link to. Access adds an entry for a linked table to the Navigation pane, displaying an icon that identifies the type of data source. (The icon includes a small arrow to indicate that the table is a linked table.)

> ➤ **To link to a table in another Access database**

1. On the **External Data** tab, click Access in the **Import & Link** group.
2. In the **Get External Data** dialog box, click **Link to the data source by creating a linked table**.
3. Click **Browse** to locate the source database, and then click **OK**.
4. In the **Link Tables** dialog box, select the table or tables you want to link to, and then click **OK**.

Linking to an Excel worksheet or a text file

The first step in linking to a worksheet or a text file is to click the Excel or Text File command in the Import & Link group. In the Get External Data dialog box, click Link To The Data Source By Creating A Linked Table, and then find the file you want to link to. Access provides a wizard (the Link Text wizard, for example) that functions much like the wizards you follow to import data into a new table.

> **See Also** For more information about using the import wizards, see the "Importing data from Excel" and "Importing text files" subtopics of the "Importing data into a table" topic earlier in this section.

➤ **To link to a text file**

1. On the **External Data** tab, click **Text File** in the **Import & Link** group.

2. In the **Get External Data** dialog box, click **Link to the data source by creating a linked table**, click **Browse** to locate the source file, and then click **OK**.

3. In the **Link Text** wizard, specify the format for the file you are importing (**Delimited** or **Fixed Width**), and then click **Next**.

4. Choose the delimiting character or specify column breaks (depending on the format). Select **First Row Contains Field Names** if this option applies.

5. Click **Next** to work through the remaining pages to set field options, designate a primary key, and name the table.

6. Click **Finish**, and then click **OK** in the **Link Text** wizard message box that confirms the table was linked.

➤ **To link to an Excel worksheet or named range**

1. On the **External Data** tab, click **Excel** in the **Import & Link** group.

2. In the **Get External Data** dialog box, click **Link to the data source by creating a linked table**, click **Browse** to locate the source file, and then click **OK**.

3. In the **Link Spreadsheet** wizard, select the worksheet or named range that has the data you want to link to, and then click **Next**.

4. Specify whether the first column of the data includes column headings, and then click Next.

5. Enter a name for the linked table.

6. Click **Finish**, and then click **OK** in the **Link Spreadsheet** wizard message box that confirms the table was linked.

Managing linked tables

If a source file you have linked to is moved to a different location, you can update the link by using the Linked Table Manager dialog box. This dialog box lists each table linked to in the current database. Select the check box for the link you want to update and then click OK; Access displays the Select New Location dialog box, where you can locate the file again. Select the Always Prompt For New Location check box if you want Access to prompt you when a linked file has been moved.

➤ **To manage linked tables**

1. On the **External Data** tab, in the **Import & Link** group, click **Linked Table Manager**.

2. In the **Linked Table Manager** dialog box, select the check box for the table or tables whose link you want to update, and then click **OK**. If the source file is not in the original location, Access displays the **Select New Location** dialog box.

3. In the **Select New Location** dialog box, find the new location for the file, select the file, and then click **Open**.

4. In the **Linked Table Manager** message box, click **OK**.

Creating tables in Access web apps

As explained in Chapter 1, "Create and manage databases," when you create an Access web app (by using a template or the Custom Web App option), Access displays the Add Tables page. Entries for any tables the template provides by default appear on the Navigation pane. You can use the search box on the Add Tables page to locate a table template and add that table to the web app. Click the entry for the table you want to add.

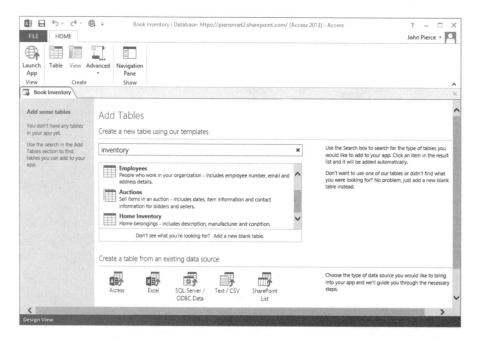

When you click the link to add a new blank table, Access assigns a default name (such as *Table1*) and displays the table in Design view, with an ID column defined and set as the table's primary key. The Table Tools Design tool tab for a web app has fewer options than a desktop database has. It includes commands for adding and deleting fields, creating an index, modifying lookup fields, opening the Expression Builder, and creating a table validation rule.

The Design tool tab also includes an Events group where you can define a series of actions and operations that occur automatically when a record is inserted, updated, or deleted. These events are similar to data macros that you can create for tables and records in a desktop database.

> **Tip** This chapter does not cover defining table events in detail, but for more information, go to the Access help system topic "Add data macros to a table event."

> **Tip** Use the icons at the bottom of the Add Tables window to import data into a web app. For more information, see the "Importing data into a table" topic earlier in this section.

Practice tasks

The practice file for these tasks is located in the MOSAccess2013\Objective2 practice file folder. You can save the results of the tasks in the same folder.

- Open the *Marketing_2* database.

- Import the *Tasks* text file to create a new table.

- Use Design view to create a table named *Status* that has the fields *StatusID* and *Status*. Set *StatusID* as the primary key. Set *Status* as a Short Text field. Create a relationship between the *Status* table and the *Tasks* table you created in the previous step.

- In the *Marketing_2* database, link to the *Employees* table and the *Compensation* tables in the *Employees* database.

2.2 Format tables

This section covers various aspects of how you can format a table. Here, *format* doesn't mean applying fonts, styles, and other text effects to alter the appearance of the data. Access does provide formatting tools, but you most often use this type of formatting in forms and reports. Instead, formatting a table involves activities such as hiding or freezing fields to make a large datasheet easier to view, and adding a Total row to display summary values for fields (a count of how many orders are recorded, for example, or the total sum or average amount of payments you've received). This section also explores options for data formats, such as using a short date or a long date in a field.

Hiding fields in tables

When a table includes more than 10 or so fields, you might not be able to easily view all the fields with the table open in Datasheet view. To avoid the need to scroll to view a field, you can hide fields you don't need to refer to. You can also freeze fields so that a specific field (or fields) remains in view as you scroll.

To hide a field, right-click the column heading for that field, and then click Hide Fields. Drag through two or more column headings to hide multiple fields, or hold down the Shift key and click column headings to select more than one adjacent field.

To show hidden fields, right-click a column heading, and then click Unhide Fields. In the Unhide Columns dialog box, select the check box for each field you want to show.

> **Tip** You can also use the Unhide Columns dialog box to hide fields. Display the dialog box by clicking Unhide Fields on the shortcut menu, and then clear the check boxes for any fields you want to hide.

To freeze a field or set of fields, right-click the column heading for the field or fields, and then click Freeze Fields. (Press Shift and click or drag to select more than one adjacent field.) You can freeze a field whose column is at any position in the datasheet. Access moves the column or columns you freeze to the far left of the datasheet, placing the column or columns before any others.

To unfreeze fields, right-click a column heading, and then click Unfreeze All Fields. If Access moved a field to the first position in the table, unfreezing the field does not return this column (or columns) to its original position in the table. You need to drag the column heading to place the column where you want it in the table.

➤ **To hide and unhide fields**

1. In the Navigation pane, double-click the table to open it in Datasheet view.
2. Right-click the column heading for the fields you want to hide, and then click **Hide Fields**.
3. To show hidden fields, right-click a column heading, and then click **Unhide Fields**.
4. In the **Unhide Columns** dialog box, select the check boxes for the fields you want to show.

➤ **To freeze and unfreeze fields**

1. In the Navigation pane, double-click the table to open it in Datasheet view.
2. Right-click the column heading of the fields you want to freeze, and then click **Freeze Fields**.
3. To unfreeze fields, right-click a column heading, and then click **Unfreeze All Fields**.

Changing data formats

When you assign certain data types to a field, you can apply a format that affects how the data in the field is displayed. Date/Time fields and Currency fields are examples. For a Currency field, you can specify the Currency format, which shows the values with a dollar sign ($) and separates thousands with a comma. Other currency formats include Euro (which uses the euro symbol instead of a dollar sign), Fixed (which removes the dollar sign and thousands separator), and Standard (no monetary symbol, but thousands are separated with a comma). Similar format options are available for a Number field.

In Design view, you can view a list of formats for a field by opening the list in the Format property box.

When you have a table open in Datasheet view, a list of formats you can apply to a field appears in the Formatting group on the Table Tools Fields tool tab. Select the column heading for a field, and then select a format from the Format list. For Number and Currency fields, you can also use the set of formatting options below the format list.

➤ **To change a field's data format in Datasheet view**

1. Open the table in Datasheet view.

2. Click the column heading for a field.

3. In the **Formatting** group on the **Table Tools Fields** tool tab, select the format you want.

> **Tip** The Format list is not available when you select a field without formatting options.

Adding a Total row

As Chapter 3, "Create queries," describes, one use of a query is to summarize data—that is, to count the number of records in a query or calculate the aggregate value of a Number or Currency field. You can also summarize data in a table by adding a Total row to display summary values for one or more fields. A Total row uses built-in functions such as Sum and Count. To apply Sum to a field, the field's data type must be set to Number or Currency. For fields that don't use a numeric data type (such as a text field), you can apply the Count function. In numeric fields, you can also apply the functions Average, Maximum, Minimum, Standard Deviation, and Variance.

➤ **Add a Total row to a table**

1. In the Navigation pane, double-click the table (or right-click the table, and then click **Open**).

2. On the **Home** tab, in the **Records** group, click **Totals**.

3. For each column in the **Total** row where you want a total to appear, click in the column, and then select the function you want to apply.

4. To remove the **Total** row, click **Totals** in the **Records** group.

Adding table descriptions

One of the properties you can define for a table is Description. Adding a description is another step you can take to document the objects and logic in your database.

You can add a description either in Design view (by displaying the table's property sheet) or in a table's Properties dialog box, which you open by right-clicking the table in the Navigation pane and then clicking Table Properties.

A command named Table Properties also appears on the Table Tools Table tool tab when a table is open in Datasheet view. The command in this location opens a dialog box in which you can set other table properties, including settings for how a table is sorted and filtered by default and the table's orientation. The Orientation property specifies the reading sequence of the data in Datasheet view. The default in most versions of Access is Left-to-Right; for languages that read right to left, the default is Right-to-Left. The Read Only When Disconnected property (set to No by default) affects whether you can update records in a table that's linked to a SharePoint list when you're working offline.

These and other table properties are also available in the table's property sheet, which you can open from the Show/Hide group on the Table Tools Design tool tab when you have the table open in Design view.

Use these dialog boxes to specify table properties, such as a description, a default filter, and an orientation

Opens from the Navigation pane   Opens from the Table Tools Table tool tab

➤ **To add a description and set other table properties**

1. Right-click the table in the Navigation pane, and then click **Table Properties**.
2. Enter a description in the **Description** box.
3. Open the table in Datasheet view.
4. On the **Table Tools Table** tool tab, click **Table Properties**.
5. In the **Enter Table Properties** dialog box, specify the settings you need.

Renaming tables

Renaming a table requires only a couple of steps, but renaming a table or any of the objects in your database can produce results you don't expect. You can use the Name AutoCorrect options in the Access Options dialog box (on the Current Database page) to help manage any unintended consequences.

The names of objects are used to define a form's record source, for example. If a table named *Tasks* is specified as a form's record source and you rename that table, the form can't display task records unless its Record Source property is updated.

By default, two name AutoCorrect options are selected: Track Name AutoCorrect Info and Perform Name AutoCorrect. With these settings, Access keeps track of when an object's name changes and updates references to the object so that forms (and queries and reports) continue to retrieve the records they're designed to. You can also select the option Log Name AutoCorrect Changes to have Access maintain a log of the changes it makes.

➤ **To rename a table**

1. Right-click the table in the Navigation pane.

2. Click **Rename**, and then enter the name you want to use.

Practice tasks

The practice file for these tasks is located in the MOSAccess2013\Objective2 practice file folder. You can save the results of the tasks in the same folder.

- Open the *Northwind* sample database from the practice file folder. Close the *Home* form before continuing.

- Open the *Customers* table in Datasheet view. Practice hiding, unhiding, freezing, and unfreezing fields to set up different views of the table.

- Open the *Orders* table in Datasheet view. Change the format for the *Order Date* field to *Medium Date.*

- Add a *Total* row to the *Orders* table. Use the *Total* row to display the number of orders that shipped.

- Add a description to the *Customers* table.

- Check the settings for the Name AutoCorrect options in the Access Options dialog box. Rename the *Customers* table *Clients.* Experiment by clearing the name AutoCorrect options and the renaming the table again. Open a customer-related form.

2.3 Manage records

You can manage the records in a table in Datasheet view. This section describes how to add, update, and delete records, and also how to find, sort, and filter records when you need to work with records that match specific criteria. The section also describes how you can append records to an existing table.

Adding, updating, and deleting records

The actions of adding a record, updating a record's value, or deleting a record can be affected by table relationships and whether a relationship enforces referential integrity. You can't add or change a record in a table when a related record is required in another table—for example, you can't add the details of an order to the Order Details table unless a record for that order exists in the Orders table. Similarly, Access prevents you from deleting a record in one table (a task, for example) that creates orphan records in another table (issues related to that task).

In a relationship that enforces referential integrity, the Cascade Update Related Fields and Cascade Delete Related Records options in the Edit Relationships dialog box determine how Access manages records you update or delete. In the *Northwind* sample database, for example, in the relationship between the Orders and Order Details tables, Cascade Delete Related Records is selected. If you delete a record from the Orders table, related records will be deleted from the Order Details table.

> **See Also** For information about table relationships and referential integrity, see section 1.2, "Manage relationships and keys."

When relationships don't restrict how you manage records (when you are first entering data in a table, for example), you work with the Records group on the Home tab to create new records, save records, and delete records. To add a record, you can also simply enter it in the last row in the table, which is labeled New. (Clicking New in the Records group on the Home tab takes you to this row.) To update a value in a record, click in the field whose value you want to change, and then enter the new value or select the value in a list if the field provides one.

Also keep in mind that you can save a record without entering data for each field, but some fields might be required. You can't save a record without entering a value in a required field.

➤ **To work with records in Datasheet view**

1. In the **Records** group, on the **Home** tab, click **New**.

2. Enter the values for each field that defines the record.

3. In the **Records** group, click **Save**.

4. To update the value for a field, select the field, and then enter the new value.

5. To delete a value from a specific field, select the value, and then click **Delete** in the **Records** group.

6. To delete a record, click the record selector (at the left edge of the table), and then click **Delete Record** in the **Records** group.

Appending records

When you import data from Excel or a text file, you can choose an option to append records to an existing table. (This option reads Append A Copy Of The Records To The Table). Access adds the records in the source data to the table you specify. The steps for importing the data are then essentially the same as when you import data into a new table.

> **See Also** For more information about importing data, see the "Importing data into a table" topic in section 2.1, "Create a table."

To avoid errors when you append data, the organization of the external data source should match the structure of the table you are appending records to. For example, in an Excel worksheet that does not contain column headings, the position and the type of data need to match the field order and data types in the destination table. When column headings are present, the name and data type for each column must match the corresponding fields (although the order of the columns and fields do not need to match). Also check whether the source data contains any fields not included in the table. If the source data does contain other fields, you should add these fields to the destination table or specify to skip them for the import process. The destination table can have fields not defined in the source data, provided those fields have their Required property set to No and the fields do not contain any validation rules that prohibit null values.

The source data must include data that is compatible with the table's primary key, and the data in that column must be unique. You receive an import error message if a primary key value in the source data matches one already defined in the destination table. Also, if the Indexed property of any field in the destination table is set to Yes (No Duplicates), the source data must include unique values for that field.

> **Important** You cannot choose the option to append records for all the formats Access can import. You can choose this option for Excel, for a text file, or for an Outlook folder, for example. The option is not available for an XML file or for a SharePoint list.

➤ **To append records to a table in the current database**

1. On the **External Data** tab, click the command for the data source you want to import.

2. In the **Get External Data** dialog box, click **Append a copy of the records to the table**, and then select the table you want to append records to.

3. Click **Browse** to locate the file with the source data, and then click **OK**.

4. Follow the steps in the import wizard (if Access provides one) to import and append the data.

5. In the **Get External Data** dialog box, select **Save import steps** if you want to save the steps in this operation.

Finding, sorting, and filtering data

Over time, a database grows to include thousands of records. Locating a specific record by scrolling through a table's datasheet (or by using a form) is inefficient in circumstances like this. To locate a record or a group of records that share specific criteria, you can use commands to find, sort, and filter records in Datasheet view.

Finding records

The Find and Replace commands in the Find group (on the Home tab) open the Find And Replace dialog box. (You can also right-click a column heading in the datasheet and then click Find.)

After you enter the value you're looking for in the dialog box's Find What box, you can refine the search for this record as follows:

- Use the Look In list to specify whether Access should search the current field or the entire table (the Current Document option).

- The Match list provides three options: Whole Field, Any Part Of Field, and Start Of Field:

  - Choose the Whole Field option (the default setting) to find records with values that match the entire text string you enter in the Find What box. For example, if you enter **Blue**, Access does not find records whose value is Light Blue, Dark Blue, or Navy Blue.

  - Choose Any Part Of Field in the Match list if you want to locate records that contain the text string you enter in any part of the field. If you enter **Blue** with this option selected, Access finds records for Blue, Light Blue, Dark Blue, and Navy Blue (and those like them).

○ Click Start Of Field to locate records that begin with a specific string of char-acters—all records whose Description field starts with "Spa," for example, to find the records for Spanish olive oil, spaghetti, and sparkling water.

- Use the Search list to specify whether Access should search down, up, or all (both directions).

- Click the Match Case option to implement a case-sensitive search.

- The Search Fields As Formatted option is enabled when you are searching a field that has a particular format or an input mask. With this option selected, Access searches the data as it is displayed instead of how Access stores it. This option is particularly useful in date and time fields.

Use the Replace tab in the Find And Replace dialog box if you want to insert new data for the data Access finds. You can replace all instances of the data (click Replace All) or a single instance (click Replace).

➤ **To find records**

1. In the Navigation pane, double-click the table to open it in Datasheet view.

2. On the **Home** tab, click **Find**.

3. In the **Find and Replace** dialog box, enter the text you want to find in the **Find What** box.

4. In the **Look In** list, select **Current field** or **Current document** (which refers to the entire table).

5. In the **Match** list, select **Whole Field**, **Any Part of Field**, or **Start of Field**.

6. In the **Search** list, select **All**, **Up**, or **Down**.

7. Select **Match Case** to perform a case-sensitive search.

8. Select **Search Fields As Formatted** if you want to search the data as it is formatted in the datasheet.

9. Click **Find Next**.

Sorting records

On the Home tab, in the Sort & Filter group, the Ascending and Descending commands sort a table's records by a field you select. Click the column heading in the datasheet (or click a cell in that column), and then click the command for the sort order you want to apply. To return a table to the default sort order, click Remove Sort.

You can also sort a table by multiple columns. For example, you can sort a table on the Launch Date field in ascending order, and the Campaign Budget field in descending order, to determine how budgets compare for each campaign scheduled to launch over a period of time. When you sort by multiple fields, apply the second, or *inner*, sort first (in this case, budgets in descending order).

Sorting commands are also available when you click Filter in the Sort & Filter group. A text field provides the commands Sort A To Z or Sort Z To A. Number fields have the commands Sort Smallest To Largest or Sort Largest To Smallest, and date fields use Sort Oldest To Newest and Sort Newest To Oldest. You can also apply these sorting options when you right-click in a column or when you click the arrow that appears to the right of a field's name.

For more advanced sorts, click Advanced in the Sort & Filter group, and then click Advanced Filter/Sort. Access displays a window with a list of the table's fields in the top pane and a grid in the bottom pane. (If you open this window when a sort order is applied, the grid shows the field and sort criteria specified.)

> **Tip** The Advanced Filter/Sort window is very much like the query design window. For more information, see the "Using the Query Designer" topic in section 3.1, "Create a query."

To sort a table by multiple fields,
drag fields from the field list to the Field row
in the grid, and then specify a sort order

To sort by a field, drag it from the field list to the Field row in the grid. In the Sort row, specify Ascending or Descending.

To create a multiple-field sort in the Advanced Filter/Sort window, drag a second field from the field list to the Field row in the grid. In the Sort row, select Ascending or Descending. After you arrange the fields you want to sort by, click the Toggle Filter button in the Sort & Filter group, and Access displays the table in Datasheet view sorted as you specified. Click Remove Sort to return the table to its default sort order.

➤ **To sort records from the Home tab**

1. In the Navigation pane, double-click the table to open it in Datasheet view.

2. Click the field you want to sort by.

3. On the **Home** tab, in the **Sort & Filter** group, click **Ascending** or **Descending**.

➤ **To sort records by using a shortcut menu**

1. In the Navigation pane, double-click the table to open it in Datasheet view.

2. Right-click the field you want to sort by, and then click the command for the sort order you want to use. (The command names depend on the field's data type.)

➤ **To set up and apply an advanced sort**

1. In the Navigation pane, double-click the table to open it in Datasheet view.

2. On the **Home** tab, in the **Sort & Filter** group, click **Advanced**, and then click **Advanced Filter/Sort**.

3. In the **Advanced Filter/Sort** window, drag the field or fields you want to sort by to the **Field** row in the grid.

4. In the **Sort** row, select the sort order you want to use.

5. In the **Sort & Filter** group, click **Toggle Filter** to sort the records.

6. Click **Remove Sort** to return the table to its default sort order.

Filtering records

By applying a filter to a table in Datasheet view, you can select the specific set of records you want to review, such as all orders placed on or after a specific date, or all amounts less than or greater than a target.

Access provides many ways to filter records. For example, click in the column for the field you want to filter, and then click Filter in the Sort & Filter group. Access displays a menu with the values in that field. Clear the Select All check box, select the check box for each value you want to view, and then click OK to apply the filter. Click the Toggle Filter button to display all the records in the table again. (You can display the same menu by clicking the arrow to the right of a column name.)

Another way to filter is to filter by selection. Select a value or a portion of a value to use as the filter criterion. In the Sort & Filter group, click Selection, and then choose one of the expressions Access provides. Expressions for text fields include Equals *Value*, Does Not Equal *Value*, and Contains *Value*. For date fields, the expressions include Equals *Date*, Does Not Equal *Date*, On Or Before *Date*, On Or After *Date*, and Between, which lets you specify a date range to use as the filter. For Number fields, Less Than Or Equal To and Greater Than Or Equal To options are included along with Equals and Does Not Equal.

> **Tip** You can filter progressively by selection to hone in on a particular set of records. For example, the first time you apply a filter, the criteria you use might reduce 200 records to 75. Filter the remaining records by using different criteria to review a smaller subset.

Similar filtering expressions appear on the menu Access displays when you right-click in a column. The shortcut menu also includes a command that provides additional filters based on the field's data type. The Text Filters command displays the Equals, Does Not Equal, Begins With, Does Not Begin With, Ends With, and Does Not End With filters. Choose a filter, and then specify the criteria in the Custom Filter dialog box that Access displays.

The Date Filters commands include options such as Before, After, and Between, in addition to Next Week, Last Week, Year To Date, and many others. You can also choose All Dates In Period and then choose a period such as Quarter 1 or a specific month of the year.

The Advanced button in the Sort & Filter group provides other options for applying a filter, including Filter By Form and Advanced Filter/Sort. When you click Filter By Form, Access opens a blank datasheet with the names of the table's fields at the top of each column. On the Look For tab, enter the filter criteria in the field you want to use as the filter's criterion. You can choose a value in more than one field to create an AND condition—for example, a filter that displays records for products whose size equals Large *and* whose color equals Blue. Click the Or tab at the bottom of the window to set up additional values for the filter. If you specify filter criteria on the Or tab, Access returns records that match either the criteria specified on the Look For tab or on the Or tab.

In the Advanced Filter/Sort window, use the grid below the list of table fields to build filter criteria. Select a field in the Field row in the grid (or drag a field from the field list to the grid), and then define the criteria you want to apply. To define the criteria, you enter an expression such as **="France"** for a text value, or **>#2/1/2004#** for a date field.

Filters are similar to Access queries in that they define criteria that display a subset of a table's records. The similarity between filters and queries is apparent when you experiment with two other commands on the Advanced Filter/Sort menu: Load From Query and Save As Query.

To use a query you've defined as a filter, click Load From Query. In the Applicable Filter dialog box, select a query and then click OK. Access shows the query's fields and criteria in the design grid area of the Advanced Filter/Sort window. Click Toggle Filter to apply the filter to the table.

You can use the Save As Query command to save a filter as a query that you can then run independently or include in other queries.

> **Tip** Use the Clear Grid command to remove any criteria from the grid.

➤ **To filter by a field in Datasheet view**

1. Select the field you want to filter by, and then click **Filter** in the **Sort & Filter** group on the **Home** tab.

2. In the menu that Access displays, clear the check box for **Select All**.

3. Select the check box for each field value you want to view, and then click **OK**.

➤ **To filter by selection in Datasheet view**

1. Select the value or the portion of a value you want to use as the filter.

2. In the **Sort & Filter** group on the **Home** tab, click **Selection**.

3. In the menu Access displays, select the expression for the filter (**Equals**, **Does Not Equal**, or another filtering option).

4. Click **Toggle Filter** to remove the filter from the table.

➤ **To filter by form**

1. In the **Sort & Filter** group on the **Home** tab, click **Advanced** and then click **Filter By Form**.

2. In the **Filter by Form** window, on the **Look for** tab, enter the value in the field or fields you want to use as the filter.

3. Click the **Or** tab to set up OR conditions.

4. In the **Sort & Filter** group, click **Toggle Filter** to apply the filter. Click **Toggle Filter** again to remove the filter.

➤ **To create an advanced filter**

1. On the **Home** tab, in the **Sort & Filter** group, click **Advanced,** and then click **Advanced Filter/Sort**.

2. In the **Advanced Filter/Sort** window, in the **Field** row in the grid, select the fields you want to use in the filter.

3. In the **Criteria** row, specify the expression to use in the filter.

4. In the **Sort & Filter** group, click **Toggle Filter** to apply the filter. Click **Toggle Filter** again to remove the filter.

➤ **To use a query as a filter**

1. On the **Home** tab, in the **Sort & Filter** group, click **Advanced** and then click **Advanced Filter/Sort**.

2. Click **Advanced** again, and then choose **Load from Query**.

3. In the **Applicable Filter** dialog box, select the query you want to use as a filter, and then click **OK**.

4. In the **Sort & Filter** group, click **Toggle Filter** to apply the filter. Click **Toggle Filter** again to remove the filter.

➤ **To save a filter as a query**

1. On the **Home** tab, in the **Sort & Filter** group, click **Advanced**, and then click **Advanced Filter/Sort**.

2. In the **Advanced Filter/Sort** window, in the **Field** row in the grid, select the fields you want to use in the filter.

3. In the **Criteria** row, specify the expression to use in the filter.

4. Click **Advanced**, and then choose **Save As Query**.

5. Enter a name for the query in the **Save As Query** dialog box, and then click **OK**.

Practice tasks

The practice files for these tasks are located in the MOSAccess2013\Objective2 practice file folder. You can save the results of the tasks in the same folder.

*   Open the *Marketing_2* database and then open the *CampaignExpenses* table in Datasheet view.

*   Sort the table's records in ascending order by using the *Description* field, and then remove the sort.

*   Sort the *Description* field in descending order and the *AmountSpent* field in ascending order.

*   Filter the *ExpenseType* field to show only records that equal the value *Travel*.

*   Create an advance filter by using criteria that filters for expense types equal to *Production*, and the amount spent greater than $800.

2.4 Create and modify fields

The beginning of this chapter described how to work in Design view or Datasheet view to create tables. This section expands on how tables are defined by describing details about fields—how you create them (and delete them), and how you work with field properties to fine-tune a table's design. You examine how to set field sizes and captions, input masks, field validation rules, and default values, in addition to how to increment the value in a field automatically and how to change a field's data type.

You can accomplish most of the tasks described in this section with the table open in Design view or in Datasheet view.

Adding and deleting fields

In Design view, add a field by entering the field name in the first blank row, or use the Insert Rows command in the Tools group (on the Table Tools Design tool tab) to add the field between two fields that are already defined. (A row is inserted above the selected row.) Use the Delete Rows command in the Tools group to remove a field from a table—this command is also available when you right-click a row and display the shortcut menu. If you delete a field that contains data, Access prompts you to confirm this action, warning that you will permanently delete the field and its data.

When a table is open in Datasheet view, you add and delete fields by working with commands in the Add & Delete group on the Table Tools Fields tool tab. A field you insert appears to the right of the field selected in the table. The Add & Delete group provides options that correspond to Access data types. Use the Short Text, Number, Currency, Date/Time, and Yes/No options to insert a field and apply that data type. Click More Fields to open a menu that provides additional data types, including Attachment, Hyperlink, and Long Text, plus a variety of formats for the Number, Date/Time, and Yes/No data types.

The last category in the More Fields list is the Quick Start group. Similar to the Quick Start application parts described in Chapter 1, "Create and manage databases," these Quick Start items contain one or more fields that are assigned appropriate data types. Add Quick Start items (also known as *data type application parts*) to a table to define a group of related fields.

In fields provided by Quick Start data types, many field properties are set so that you can start using the fields to capture data without additional work. For example, the Address item adds fields named Address, City, State Province, ZIP Postal, and Country Region. (You can rename the fields to fit your particular database.) The Payment Type item inserts a lookup field that includes the list Cash, Credit Card, Check, and In-Kind.

> **See Also** For more information about setting field properties, see the "Working with field properties" topic later in this section.

You can create your own Quick Start data types by selecting the field or fields you want to use and then clicking Save Selection As New Data Type at the bottom of the More Fields list. In the Create New Data Types From Fields dialog box, enter a name and a description for the new data type, and then select a category (or enter a new category name).

> **Tip** Data type application parts that you create are stored in the default location for Access database templates, using the .accft file name extension. You can share these files so that colleagues and coworkers can also work with the data types you create.

You can also insert and manage fields in Datasheet view by using commands on the shortcut menu that appears when you right-click a column heading. Click Insert Field to add a column to the left of the column heading you clicked. To define the data type for this field, type a value in the field so that Access applies a data type, or use the Data

Type list in the Formatting group on the Fields tool tab to select the data type and format you want. The controls available in this group depend on the data type you select.

> **Tip** You can also insert a field in a table that's open in Datasheet view by clicking in the Click To Add column, which is displayed at the right of the columns already defined for the table.

To rename a field, double-click the column heading for the field, or right-click the heading and then click Rename Field.

> **See Also** For information about renaming database objects, see the "Renaming tables" topic in section 2.2, "Format tables."

To delete a field from a table in Datasheet view, click the Delete button in the Add & Delete group, or right-click a field's column heading and then click Delete Field. Keep in mind that Access prevents you from deleting a field that is part of a relationship and displays a message box informing you that you must delete the relationship first.

➤ **To add a field in Datasheet view**

1. On the **Table Tools Fields** tool tab, in the **Add & Delete** group, click the data type for the field you want to insert. Click **More Fields** to display an extended list of data types.

2. In the column heading row, enter a name for the field.

➤ **To insert a Quick Start data type**

1. On the **Fields** tool tab, in the **Add & Delete** group, click **More Fields**, and then scroll down to display the **Quick Start** group.

2. Select the **Quick Start** data type you want to insert.

➤ **To define a custom data type application part**

1. In the datasheet, select the field or fields you want to include in the custom data type.

2. On the **Fields** tool tab, in the **Add & Delete** group, click **More Fields**, and then click **Save Selection as New Data Type**.

3. In the **Create New Data Type from Fields** dialog box, enter a name and description for the custom data type. Select an entry in the **Category** list, or enter the name for a new category.

➤ **To rename a field in Datasheet view**

1. Right-click the column heading for the field, and then click **Rename Field**.

2. In the highlighted area, enter the new name for the field.

➤ **To delete a field in Datasheet view**

1. Right-click the column heading for the field, and then click **Delete Field**.

2. Click **Yes** in the prompt that Access displays to confirm that you want to delete the field.

Working with field properties

Fields are defined not only by their name and data type. *Field properties* add to the definition of a field by specifying a format (as in Date/Time fields), whether a field is required, whether Access creates an index for that field, the field's default value, and other information.

Field properties can be set in Design view or in Datasheet view. In Datasheet view, commands related to field properties are organized in three groups on the Table Tools Fields tool tab: Properties, Formatting, and Field Validation. Be sure to select a field in the datasheet before you set or modify the field's properties.

This section describes how you work with several field properties in Datasheet view, what additional properties are available in Design view, and more details about how to modify fields in a table.

Adding validation rules to fields

The data type you assign to a field prevents some erroneous data entry. For example, enter the text *"test"* in a Date/Time field, and Access displays a warning telling you that the value does not match the Date/Time data type. You can define a validation rule for a field to further control the data a user can enter. (Validation rules don't apply for all types of fields. You use them most often for fields that use the Short Text, Number, Currency, or Date/Time data types.)

A simple validation rule might compare the value of a field to one or more constants. For example, enter the expression **<1000** as a field validation rule to ensure that the field contains no values greater than 1,000. Be sure to enclose text strings in quotation marks, and enclose dates with pound signs (#). For example, you can create a validation rule that specifies a list of valid values for a product size field by using the expression *"Large" OR "Medium" OR "Small"*. For a Date/Time field, the expression *BETWEEN #1/1/2013#* and *#12/31/2013#* sets the field validation rule so that only dates in calendar year 2013 are valid.

You can use the LIKE operator and wildcard characters to specify a valid pattern. For example, for a five-digit US ZIP Code, use the expression *LIKE "#####"*.

In Design view, use the Validation Text property to enter an error message that Access displays when invalid data is entered in the field. In Datasheet view, click Field Validation Message to define the message.

> **See Also** For information about using the Expression Builder, see the "Getting help from the Expression Builder" sidebar in section 3.3, "Utilize calculated fields and grouping within queries."

➤ **To add a field validation rule**

1. Open the table in Datasheet view.

2. On the **Table Tools Fields** tool tab, click **Validation**, **Field Validation Rule**.

3. In the Expression Builder, enter the expression that defines the rule, and then click **OK**.

4. On the **Fields** tool tab, click **Validation**, **Field Validation Message**.

5. In the **Enter Validation Message** dialog box, enter the message that Access displays if users enter invalid data.

Changing field captions

By default, a field's name identifies the field in the column heading in Datasheet view or when the field is added to a form or a report. You can enter a caption to change the display name for the field. For example, a database designer might name fields by using internal capitalization, such as *TaskName*. To make the field's name more readable on forms and reports, enter **Task Name** for the caption.

➤ **To change a field caption**

→ In Datasheet view, click **Name & Caption** in the **Properties** group (on the **Table Tools Fields** tool tab). In Design view, enter the caption in the **Caption** property box.

Changing field sizes

As described earlier in this chapter, the Field Size property for a field that uses the Short Text data type specifies the maximum number of characters that can be entered in the field. For example, suppose your company uses a six-character product code, with a combination of letters and numbers. You could set the Field Size property to **6** to ensure that no user enters more characters than are allowed.

For a Number field, the Field Size property specifies the extent of the numbers the field can contain (for example, Byte, Long Integer, and Single).

➤ **To change the field size**

→ In Datasheet view, use the **Field Size** box in the **Properties** group (on the **Table Tools Fields** tool tab) to specify the field size for a text field. In Design view, select the field size setting for a **Number** field; enter the value for a text field.

Setting default values

By using the Default Value command in Datasheet view (or the Default Value property box in Design view), you define the value that Access enters automatically for a field. For example, you might use the built-in function *Now()* in an order date field to fill in today's date when a new order is entered. You can also use a text or numerical constant as a field's default value. For example, you could set a default value for a country/region field so that the field is set automatically to the value you use most often. Likewise, if you sold certain products only with a minimum order quantity (only in units of 12, for example), you could set the Default Value property in the quantity field to reflect that amount.

➤ **To set the default value for a field**

→ In Datasheet view, click **Default Value** in the **Properties** group to open the Expression Builder. In Design view, you can enter the default value, or click the ellipsis button (...) in the **Default Value** property box to open the Expression Builder and enter the value or expression there.

Other field properties available in Datasheet view

The following list shows other field properties you can set in Datasheet view.

Properties group
- **Memo Settings** For Long Text fields, click Memo Settings, and then choose the Append Only or Rich Text option. Select Append Only if you want to retain the history of changes to a field. The Rich Text option converts the field to the Rich Text format and encodes the field's data as HTML.

- **Modify Expression** When you select a calculated field, Access enables the Modify Expression command. Use it to open the Expression Builder and revise the expression that defines the field.

- **Modify Lookups** When you select a lookup field, Access enables the Modify Lookups command. Use this command to open the Lookup wizard and define or modify the fields used to create the lookup relationship.

Field Validation group
- **Required** Select this option to require users to enter a value in the field before they can save the record.

- **Unique** Select this option if you want values in this field to be unique for all records.

- **Indexed** Indicates whether the field is indexed. Choose Yes (No Duplicates) or Yes (Duplicates OK). When you index a field, Access can search for values in that field more efficiently. You should index fields you expect to use frequently in criteria for queries, such as fields that store names for contacts, companies, or products.

Setting field properties in Design view

When you have a table open in Design view, select a field to display the current settings for its properties in the Field Properties area. In the area to the right of the list of properties, Access provides a brief description of each property and, in some cases, notes some restrictions or qualifications (such as a field using the Short Text data type can contain a maximum of 255 characters).

The list of properties in Design view includes those you can set in Datasheet view and others.

The following describes some of the additional field properties:

- **Allow Zero Length** Set this property to Yes or No depending on whether you want to allow zero-length strings in this field. A *zero-length string* is essentially a known empty value, which you might use to indicate that a user has no preference about the value in the field or that the value does not apply. (By contrast, a *null value* indicates an unknown empty value.)

- **Unicode Compression** When you set this property to Yes, Access stores compressed characters by using fewer bytes, which saves space in the database.

- **IME Mode and IME Sentence Mode** These properties apply to computers that run Windows using Asian languages.

- **Text Align** Specifies how text is aligned in the field. You can choose from General (the default), Left, Center, Right, and Distribute. The Distribute option spreads the data evenly over the field.

For fields using the Date/Time data type, you can also set the Show Date Picker property. Use the For Dates option to show a date picker for a field, or choose Never to hide it. For fields using the Long Text data type, use the Text Format property to specify Plain Text or Rich Text. The Rich Text option provides more formatting. For fields using the Long Text or Hyperlink data types, set the Append Only property to Yes if you want to retain the history of changes to these fields. And for a calculated field, you can use the Expression property to compose the expression that performs the calculation and then choose a data type for the result in the Result Type property.

➤ **To set and update field properties in Design view**

1. In the Navigation pane, right-click the table, and then click **Design View**.
2. Select the field whose properties you want to set.
3. In the **Field Properties** area, specify the value for the properties or select an option in the list Access provides.

Changing field data types

In building a table, the best approach is to set the data type for a field once and not change it. Especially after data has been added to a table, changing a field's data type can be problematic. For example, if you change the data type for a Date/Time field to a Number field, the dates are converted to their serial value (12/31/2013 becomes 41639). Access can handle the conversion of dates to numbers (and back to dates), but other data types don't work as smoothly. Access displays a warning if you change a field's data type from Long Text to Short Text, telling you that some data will be lost.

➤ **To change a field's data type**

→ In Design view, select the new value in the **Data Type** list. In Datasheet view, select the new setting in the **Data Type** list on the **Field** tool tab's **Formatting** group.

Configuring fields to auto-increment

Assign the AutoNumber data type to a field to have Access add a unique number in that field as you add records to a table. AutoNumber is often assigned to an ID field that is used as the table's primary key.

A table can include only one AutoNumber field whose Field Size property is set to Long Integer. (You can use the AutoNumber data type for other fields if the Field Size property is set to Replication ID.) In Design view, check the setting for the New Values property for an AutoNumber field. The default setting is Increment, which means Access assigns numbers sequentially. The Random setting produces random numbers for new records. You might use the Random setting to create unique order IDs.

Using input masks

An input mask defines a specific pattern for the data in a field. Adding an input mask to a field assists users with entering data correctly. Access provides input masks for data such as phone numbers, US Social Security numbers, ZIP Codes, passwords, and date formats.

Important An input mask doesn't not affect how data is stored. A field's data type and other properties define that format. An input mask affects only whether the data has been entered in a format Access will accept.

The Input Mask wizard lists the input masks available for a specific data type. For a Date/Time field, Access provides entries such as Long Time, Short Date, and Medium Date. For fields that use the Short Text data type, the list includes input masks for phone numbers, ZIP Codes, and other sorts of data.

To set up an input mask, click in the Input Mask property box and then click the ellipsis to run the Input Mask wizard. Enter some sample data in the Try It box to view how the mask controls data entry. (For example, select the Short Date mask, and then enter a month abbreviation in the Try It box.) You can specify how an input mask is designed (by using special characters to define the mask) in the wizard's second page. In a mask, a zero (0) indicates that a user must enter a digit (from 0 through 9) in that placeholder. A nine (9) marks an optional digit. An uppercase L is used to denote a required letter. An optional letter is marked with a question mark (?). If you want to create an input mask of your own, click Edit List in the wizard, and then use the defined special characters to set up the mask.

> **See Also** You can find a complete list of special characters and how to use them in the Access help system topic "Guide data entry by using input masks."

➤ **To specify an input mask**

1. Open a table in Design view.

2. Select the field you want to work with.

3. In the **Input Mask** property box, click the ellipsis to run the **Input Mask** wizard.

4. Select the mask you want to use, or click **Edit List** to modify a built-in mask or create one of your own.

Practice tasks

The practice files for these tasks are located in the MOSAccess2013\Objective2 practice file folder. You can save the results of the tasks in the same folder.

- Open the *Marketing_2* database.

- Open the *Customers* table in Datasheet view.

- Select the fields *Company Name*, *Contact Name*, and *Contact Title*, and then create a Quick Start data type called *ContactBasics*.

- Open the *CampaignExpenses* table, and then create a validation rule for the *AmountSpent* field so that amounts entered must be less than $1,200.

- In the *CampaignExpenses* table, make the *Description* field a required field. Use the Name & Caption command to update the *Caption* property for the *DatePurchased* field so that it reads *Purchase Date*.

- Still using the *CampaignExpenses* table, create an input mask for the *DatePurchased* field.

Objective review

Before finishing this chapter, be sure you have mastered the following skills:

2.1   Create a table

2.2   Format tables

2.3   Manage records

2.4   Create and modify fields

3 Create queries

The skills tested in this section of the Microsoft Office Specialist exam for Microsoft Access 2013 relate to creating and using queries. Specifically, the following objectives are associated with this set of skills:

3.1 Create a query
3.2 Modify queries
3.3 Utilize calculated fields and grouping within queries

Queries help you manage database records, locate records that match specific criteria, and analyze data. For example, a make-table query or an append query (two types of action queries) are often used to archive records. With a select query, you can retrieve records for all orders or add criteria to select a specific set of records (for example, only orders placed within the past 90 days that exceed a certain dollar amount).

This chapter guides you in studying methods for creating queries. It also describes how to manage tables and relationships in queries. In addition, the chapter explains how to manage fields and sort records in a query, how to group and summarize values, how to create calculated fields, and how to work with expressions and operators to define query criteria.

> **Practice Files** To complete the practice tasks in this chapter, you need the practice file contained in the MOSAccess2013\Objective3 practice file folder. For more information, see "Download the practice files" in this book's Introduction.

3.1 Create a query

The Create tab in Microsoft Access 2013 includes two commands in its Queries group: Query Wizard and Query Design. The Query Wizard command leads to a choice of wizards designed to help you create different sorts of queries. These include the Simple Query wizard and the Crosstab Query wizard. The Query Design command opens the Query Designer. In the Query Designer, you add the tables and fields a query requires and define criteria that Access applies to return a specific set of records. The commands on the Query Tools Design tool tab let you refine a query and create and run queries of specific types.

The beginning of this section describes how to run a query, and how to save and delete a query. You then examine how to create various types of queries, including select queries, parameter queries, action queries, and crosstab queries. The last topic in this section shows you how to manage and join tables that a query is based on.

Running queries

The simplest way to run a query is to double-click its entry in the Navigation pane. This action displays the query's results in Datasheet view, where you can then sort and filter the records, export the query's data, and perform other operations. You can also right-click a query in the Navigation pane and then click Open to run the query.

In the Query Designer, as you add or remove fields and define criteria and other query properties, use the Run command in the Results group (on the Query Tools Design tool tab) to view the records that the query returns. You can return to Design view (by using the View menu on the Home tab), make additional modifications to the query, and then run the query again to check the effects of the changes.

➤ **To run a query**

1. In the Navigation pane, double-click the query.

2. In Design view, click **Run** on the **Query Tools Design** tool tab.

Saving and deleting queries

Access automatically saves a query you create by using one of the query wizards. When you design a query from scratch in the Query Designer, Access assigns a default name to the query (*Query1*, for example). To name and save the query, click the Save button on the Quick Access Toolbar, or click the Save command in the Backstage view.

You can use options on the Save As page in the Backstage view to create a copy of a query as a new database object (by choosing Save Object As) or as a PDF or an XPS file. The Save Object As command can be helpful if you want to experiment with a query that's already designed (by adding additional selection criteria, for example) and don't want to risk inadvertent changes to the original query.

To delete a query from a database, right-click the query in the Navigation pane, and then click Delete. Keep in mind that queries are often used as the record source for forms and reports. If you delete a query that's the basis of a form or report, you need to update the record source before you can use the form or report to view records.

➤ **To save a query**

   1. On the **Quick Access Toolbar**, click **Save**.

   2. In the **Save As** dialog box, enter a name for the query, and then click **OK**.

➤ **To delete a query**

   → In the Navigation pane, right-click the query, and then click **Delete**.

Creating select queries

A *select query* returns all or a subset of the records stored in one or more tables. When creating a select query, you specify which fields you want to use, and you can also define criteria to return a specific set of records. One simple use for a select query is to set up a record source for a mailing list. For example, by using a contacts table as the basis for the query, you could include name, address, and related fields in the query without adding fields for a contact's email address and phone number. If you're sending a mailing to contacts in specific locations, you could define criteria that limits the records the query returns to contacts in the particular cities or postal codes you designate.

Select queries (and queries of other types) also illustrate the purpose of table relationships. You can add two or more tables to a query and use their relationship to retrieve a set of records from all the tables—for example, all high-priority tasks related to projects for a particular customer, managed by a specific employee, and with a completion date within 30 days.

To create a select query, you can use the Simple Query wizard or build the query by using the Query Designer. Use the Query Designer if you want to add criteria to the query (however, the wizard does have an option that leads to the Query Designer if you need it).

Using the Simple Query wizard

To start the Simple Query wizard, click Query Wizard in the Queries group on the Create tab. In the New Query dialog box, select Simple Query Wizard. In the next step, add fields from one or more tables (or queries) to define the query you're creating.

Select a table or query
from this list box

Move available fields to
the Selected Fields list to
add them to the query

The Simple Query wizard tailors its steps based on factors such as the following:

- If you add fields from only one table and those fields store only text data (not numeric data), the third and last step is to provide a name for the query and then specify whether to open the query to view the records it returns or open the query in Design view for modification.

- If you include numeric or date fields or fields from more than one table, the wizard prompts you to create a detail query or a summary query. A *detail query* shows each individual record for the query. In a *summary query*, you can total the values in a field or determine the field's average, minimum, or maximum value.

- When date fields are present in a summary query, the wizard also prompts you to choose an option for how you want to group records by dates. For example, you can group records by month, quarter, or year.

> **See Also** For more information about summary queries and grouping records in a query, see section 3.3, "Utilize calculated fields and grouping within queries" later in this chapter.

➤ **To create a select query by using the Simple Query wizard**

   1. On the **Create** tab, in the **Queries** group, click **Query Wizard**.

   2. In the **New Query** dialog box, select **Simple Query Wizard**, and then click **OK**.

   3. In the **Simple Query** wizard, in the **Tables/Queries** list, select the first table or query you want to use for this query. From the **Available Fields** list, add the fields you want to include in the query to the **Selected Fields** list. Click the chevron button to move all the fields to the **Selected Fields** list.

   4. Repeat step 3 to include other tables or queries in the select query, and then add the fields you want to include. Click **Next**.

   5. If the query includes numeric fields or fields from more than one table, the wizard prompts you to create a detail query or a summary query. If you select the **Summary** option, click **Summary Options**, and then select the summary function you want to apply to the fields that Access lists. Click **OK** in the **Summary Options** dialog box, and then click **Next**.

   6. If prompted by the wizard, choose an option to group dates in the query.

   7. On the wizard's last page, enter a name for the query, and then choose whether to open the query to review the results or open the query in Design view.

Using the Query Designer

Use the Query Design command on the Create tab to open the Query Designer. The Query Designer displays the query design grid (below the main pane) and the Show Table dialog box.

The Show Table dialog box lists all the tables and queries in the current database. Click a tab (Tables, Queries, or Both) to select the object or objects that contain the fields you want to include in the query. Close the Show Table dialog box to start adding fields to the query.

> **Tip** Use Ctrl or Shift, respectively, to select more than one nonadjacent item or to select a group of adjacent objects.

If you need to add tables to a query later, open the query in Design view, and then click Show Table in the Query Setup group on the Query Tools Design tool tab. You can also right-click in the Query Designer's main pane (but not on a field list), and then click Show Table. If you need to remove a table from the Query Designer, right-click the table's field list, and then click Remove Table.

Drag the field lists in the Query Designer's main pane to reposition the lists and view more clearly the relationship lines that link tables. To add a field to the query, drag it from the field list to the Field row in a blank column in the design grid. (You can press Ctrl or Shift to select multiple fields.) You can also select fields from the list displayed when you click the arrow at the right of a column in the Field row. To add all the fields in a table to the query design grid, double-click the asterisk (*) at the top of the field list.

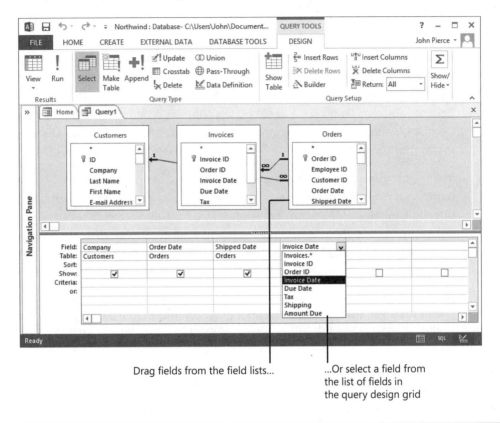

Drag fields from the field lists...

...Or select a field from the list of fields in the query design grid

> **Tip** In the query design grid, you can toggle on and off the display of table names (which appear in the Table row) by clicking Table Names in the Show/Hide group on the Design tool tab.

As mentioned earlier in this section, a select query often includes criteria that defines the subset of records the query returns when you run it. For example, to find records for customers in a specific city, add the City field to the query. In the Criteria row for that field, enter **="CityName"** (where "CityName" is the city you want to examine). You must enclose text values in quotation marks.

To specify criteria for a date field, enclose the date (or dates) in pound signs (#). You can retrieve records for orders placed between two dates by using an expression such as *Between #4/1/2014# and #4/30/2014#*. You can also use operators to retrieve records less than (<) or greater than (>) a certain numeric amount.

> **See Also** For more information about the operators you can use in a query, see the "Using operators in query criteria and expressions" topic in section 3.3, "Utilize calculated fields and grouping within queries."

When you enter criteria in the Criteria row for more than one field, the query selects only records that match the criteria in all those fields—for example, records that have a value in the Order Date field greater than 9/15/2013 *and* a value for the Company Name field of Fabrikam. If you want to set up OR criteria (to find records with a value in the Company Name field of Fabrikam *or* Contoso), enter the second criteria in the Or row (below the Criteria row).

In the Query Setup group, use the Return list (the ScreenTip reads *Top Values*) to limit the number of records the query returns. By default, a query returns all matching records, but you can select one of the preset values (5, 25, 100, 5%, or 25%) or enter a value in the list box to specify how many records you want to display. After you sort records in a query, you can use the Return list to show, for example, the top 20 orders that customers placed in the current month.

> **See Also** For more information about other commands in the Query Setup group, see the "Changing the fields in a query" topic in section 3.2, "Modify queries."

➤ To create a select query in Design view

1. On the **Create** tab, in the **Queries** group, click **Query Design**.

2. In the **Show Table** dialog box, select the tables or queries you want to use in the query. Click **Add** to add the objects to the **Query Designer**, and then click **Close**.

3. From the field lists, drag the fields you want to include in the query to the **Field** row in the query design grid. (You can also select fields from the list that Access displays when you click the arrow in the **Field** row in the query design grid.)

4. Define selection criteria for the query in the **Criteria** row and the **Or** row depending on which records you want the query to return.

5. In the **Results** group on the **Query Tools Design** tool tab, click **Run** to display the records returned by the query.

➤ **To add tables to a query**

1. Open the query in Design view.

2. On the **Design** tool tab, in the **Query Setup** group, click **Show Table**.

3. In the **Show Table** dialog box, select the tables or queries you want to add, click **Add**, and then click **Close**.

➤ **To remove a table from a query**

1. Open the query in Design view.

2. Right-click the field list for the table, and then click **Remove Table**.

Creating parameter queries

A *parameter query* (a type of select query) provides flexibility in applying criteria. Instead of adding criteria such as *="Los Angeles"* to the City field, you define a parameter for that field by using a format and prompt such as *[Enter City Name]*. With a parameter defined, you can use a single query to retrieve different sets of records based on the value you enter for the parameter.

To define a parameter, click in the Criteria row for the field you want to work with, and then enter a prompt enclosed in square brackets. For example, to create a parameter for the City field, enter ***[Enter a city name]*** or a similar prompt. When you run the query, Access displays the Enter Parameter Value dialog box, which displays the prompt you defined. Enter the value you want to use as criteria (for example, ***Chicago*** or ***Montreal*** for the city parameter), and then click OK. Access returns the set of records that match the criteria you provide.

Use brackets to define a
parameter in the Criteria row

Access prompts you for a
related value when you run
the query

> **Tip** You can also use parameters in crosstab, append, make-table, and update queries.

The second step in defining a query parameter is to specify the parameter's data type.
Click Parameters in the Show/Hide group on the Query Tools Design tool tab. In the
Query Parameters dialog box, enter the parameter name (including the brackets) just
as it appears in the design grid. In the Data Type column, select the data type (such as
Short Text or Date With Time) that matches the field you defined the parameter for.

➤ To define a parameter for a query

1. In the Navigation pane, right-click the query, and then click **Design View**.
2. Enter the parameter in the **Criteria** row, enclosing the parameter in square brackets.
3. In the **Show/Hide** group, click **Parameters**.
4. In the **Query Parameters** dialog box, in the **Parameter** column, enter the parameter exactly as it appears in the design grid. In the **Data Type** column, select the data type for the parameter, and then click **OK**.

Creating action queries

The next three sections describe different types of action queries: a make-table query, an append query, and update and delete queries. *Action queries* are often used to help manage the records in a database. For example, you can use a select query to retrieve records for all discontinued products. You can use a make-table or an append query to archive those records, and then run a delete query on the products table to remove the records for those products.

Using make-table queries

When you run a *make-table query*, Access creates a table (in the current database or in another database you designate) that's defined by the fields included in the query. A make-table query has at least a couple of functions.

- A make-table query can improve performance when you find yourself frequently running a select query that's based on several tables whose data doesn't change. Access can run the select query more quickly if it is based on a single table (created by the make-table query) instead of on multiple tables.

- You can use a make-table query to build your data archives. For example, use a make-table query to store all the orders for the past year and use the Orders table only for current orders.

A table created by a make-table query inherits field names and data types but not all settings specified for other field properties. Also, the new table does not include a primary key. You need to open the new table in Design view to update field properties and assign a primary key.

> **See Also** For information about how to set a primary key, see section 1.2, "Manage relationships and keys."

A make-table query is based on a select query. (See the previous section for details about select queries.) To be sure that the table Access creates includes the correct records, run the select query to first review the records, and then run the make-table query.

When you click Make Table in the Query Type group, Access displays the Make Table dialog box. In addition to naming the table (or selecting one from the list), you need to specify whether to include the table in the current database or in a different database. If you choose Another Database, enter the file name for the database or click Browse to select the database file.

Make Table

Make New Table

Table Name: Orders_Old

○ Current Database

◉ Another Database:

File Name: Retail Databases\Old Orders

Browse...

OK

Cancel

By clicking OK in the Make Table dialog box, you set up the query. To run the query and create the table, click Run in the Results group. After you save the make-table query, you can run it again by double-clicking the query in the Navigation pane. When you run a make-table query in the Navigation pane (after running it at least one other time to create the table), the existing table is deleted.

➤ **To create and run a make-table query**

1. Create a select query on which to base the make-table query.

> **See Also** For more information about how to create a select query, see the "Creating select queries" topic earlier in this section.

2. With the select query open in Design view, click **Run** in the **Results** group.

3. Review the records returned by the select query. In the **Views** group, click **View**, **Design View** to return the query to Design view.

4. On the **Query Tools Design** tool tab, in the **Query Type** group, click **Make Table**.

5. In the **Make Table** dialog box, enter a name for the table, and then specify whether Access should create the table in the current database or in another database. If you click **Another Database**, enter the file name or click **Browse** to locate the file, and then click **OK**.

6. In the **Results** group, click **Run**.

7. Click **Yes** in the message boxes Access displays to confirm the operation.

Appending records by using a query

Another action you can perform by using a query is to append records to a table. An *append query* is similar to a make-table query, but instead of creating a table, an append query adds records to a table that's already defined. Append queries are also useful tools for archiving records. For example, you could create a table named *Completed Projects*, and then design a query based on the Projects table and related tables to select the records you want. By running this query periodically as an append query, you create an archive of completed projects.

When you design an append query, keep in mind that the data you insert by running the query must conform to the design of the destination table. For example, the data types of matching fields must be compatible, and the source data must conform to any validation rules defined for the destination table or the fields that the table contains.

As with make-table queries, you build an append query by first defining a select query. After setting up the select query, verify that it returns the records you need by running it. If the results are correct, display the query in Design view again and then click Append in the Query Type group. In the Append dialog box, use the Table Name list to select the table you want to append records to in the current database, or click Another Database to append records to a table in a different database. (If you designate a different database, Access refreshes the Table Name list to show items from the database you specify.)

When you click OK in the Append dialog box, Access adds the Append To row to the query design grid. Based on the table you selected in the Append dialog box, Access selects and displays a matching field in the Append To row. You can change the matching fields that Access provides, but the data type and other properties of the field specified in the Append To row must be compatible with the field in the query.

Save the query, and then run it by double-clicking the query in the Navigation pane or by opening the query in Design view and then clicking Run on the Query Tools Design tool tab. After you run the query, you can open the table that the records were appended to and verify that the records were added correctly.

➤ **To create and run an append query**

1. Create a select query on which to base the append query.

> **See Also** For more information about how to create a select query, see the "Creating select queries" topic earlier in this section.

2. With the select query open in Design view, click **Run** in the **Results** group.

3. Review the records returned by the select query. In the **Views** group, click **View**, **Design View** to return the query to Design view.

4. On the **Query Tools Design** tool tab, click **Append** in the **Query Type** group.

5. In the **Append** dialog box, select the table you want to add the records to. If you click **Another Database**, enter the file name or click **Browse** to locate the file, and then click **OK**.

6. In the **Results** group, click **Run**.

7. Click **Yes** in the messages Access displays to confirm the operation.

Updating and deleting records by using a query

Action queries can also be used to update or delete records. You can use an update query to increase the values in a price field by a specified percentage or to perform date arithmetic (by adding seven days to a date, for example). A *delete query* lets you remove the set of records that meets criteria you define. You can use a delete query to remove all products marked Discontinued, for example.

To create an update query (or a delete query), start by creating a select query. After the select query is set up as you want it, click Update in the Query Type group. Access adds the Update To row to the design grid. In the Update To row for the field or fields you want to modify, enter the expression that will update the field's current values. For example, to add 30 days to the ExpirationDate field, you could enter the expression [ExpirationDate]+30 in the Update To row. When you run the update query, Access displays a message box telling you how many rows (records) will be updated. Click Yes to complete the operation.

> **Important** You cannot undo the changes made by an update query. Before you run the query, you should make a backup copy of the table whose records will be updated. Also, you can check which records will be updated before you run the query by switching the query to Datasheet view (by clicking View, Datasheet View in the Results group).

You can use a delete query to delete selected records. After setting up a select query with the fields you need to work with, click Delete in the Query Type group. Access adds the Delete row to the query grid and removes the Show and Sort rows. In the Delete row, the keyword Where appears. You need to specify criteria in the Criteria row that selects the records Access will delete. For example, you might delete all records where the Discontinued field equals Yes or all records for which the order date is older than a year from today.

When you work with delete queries, keep in mind that you might delete records you weren't expecting to. This occurs if the table you're deleting records from is related to another table, and the tables' relationship is set up to use the Cascade Delete Related Records option. You can turn off this option if necessary by clicking Relationships on the Database Tools tab and then right-clicking the relationship line linking the tables whose relationship you want to modify. Choose Edit Relationship, and then clear the check box for the Cascade Delete option. Of course, you should also create a backup of your database before running a delete query.

> **See Also** For more information about the Cascade Delete Related Records option, see section 1.2, "Manage relationships and keys."

As with an update query, you cannot use the Undo command to reverse the action of a delete query.

➤ **To create and run an update query**

1. On the **Create** tab, in the **Queries** group, click **Query Design**.

2. In the **Show Table** dialog box, select the table you want to use in the query. Click **Add** to add the table to the **Query Designer**, and then click **Close**.

3. From the table field list, drag the fields you want to include in the query to the **Field** row in the query design grid.

   Or

   Select fields from the list Access displays when you click in the **Field** row in the query design grid.

4. Define any selection criteria for the query in the **Criteria** row.

5. In the **Query Type** group, click **Update**.

6. In the **Update To** row for the field or fields you want to update, enter an expression that calculates the updated values.

7. In the **Results** group on the **Query Tools Design** tool tab, click **Run**. Click **Yes** in the warning box Access displays to complete the operation.

➤ **To create and run a delete query**

1. On the **Create** tab, in the **Queries** group, click **Query Design**.

2. In the **Show Table** dialog box, select the table you want to use in the query. Click **Add** to add the tables to the **Query Designer**, and then click **Close**.

3. From the table field list, drag the fields you want to include in the query to the **Field** row in the query design grid.
   Or

   Select fields from the list Access displays when you click in the **Field** row in the query design grid.

4. In the **Query Type** group, click **Delete**.

5. In the **Criteria** row, specify the criteria for selecting the records you want to delete.

6. In the **Results** group on the **Design** tool tab, click **Run**. Click **Yes** in the message box Access displays to complete the operation.

Viewing data in a crosstab query

A crosstab query uses *Sum*, *Avg*, or another aggregate function to group a query's results. In Datasheet view, a crosstab query looks something like a spreadsheet or a PivotTable in Microsoft Excel. The query's data is grouped by two sets of values. One set appears down the left side of the datasheet, and the other appears across the top, which is shown in this example.

> **See Also** For more information about using Sum, Avg, or other aggregate functions in a query, see the "Grouping and summarizing query records" topic in section 3.3, "Utilize calculated fields and grouping within queries."

Access provides a wizard you can use to create a crosstab query, or you can use the Query Designer to specify the fields for the query and to define the calculations you want the query to perform. When you add fields to a crosstab query, you specify which fields to use as row headings (you can use as many as three fields), which field appears in the columns across the top, and which field is used for the summary values.

Using the Crosstab Query wizard

One approach to creating a crosstab query is to use the Crosstab Query wizard to set up the basic query and then open the query in Design view to modify it. You can select fields from only one table or query when you use the Crosstab Query wizard. To work around this limitation, create a select query that includes fields from the tables you need to use, and then choose the select query as the record source when you work in the Crosstab Query wizard.

In the wizard, you need to identify the following information:

- The table or query on which to base the crosstab query.

- The field or fields (up to three fields) you want to use as row headings. If you use more than one field, Access sorts the query's records in the order in which you se-lect the fields. Keep in mind that using more than one field makes the query more difficult to read.

- The field you want to use for the column headings. It's generally good practice to choose a field that includes only a few values for the column heading field.

- The interval for grouping date/time information in the column headings (if you choose a Date/Time field for the column heading). You can choose Year, Quarter, Month, Date, or Date/Time.

- The field whose value you want to summarize and the function you want to apply. Different functions are available depending on the field's data type. This page of the wizard also includes the option Yes, Include Row Sums. Select this check box to insert a row heading in the query that uses the same field and function as the field value. A row sum also inserts a column that summarizes the remaining columns.

- The name you want to assign to the query.

When you click Finish in the Crosstab Query wizard, Access opens the query in Data-sheet view.

Creating crosstab queries in Design view

As mentioned earlier, when you use the Crosstab Query wizard, you can base the query on only a single table or a single query. When you work in Design view, you can include multiple tables or queries as the crosstab query's record source. You can also first create a select query that returns the records you want, and then use that query as the sole re-cord source for the crosstab query.

> **See Also** For information about creating select queries, see the "Creating select queries" topic earlier in this section.

To set up a crosstab query in Design view, click Query Design on the Create tab, and then use the Show Table dialog box to add the tables and queries you want to use as the record source for the crosstab query. Then, in the Query Type group, click Crosstab.

The design grid for a crosstab query contains a Total row and a Crosstab row (in addition to the Sort, Criteria, and Or rows you work with in other types of queries). You use the Crosstab row to specify which field or fields to use as row headings, which field to use for the query's column headings, and which field to summarize for the query's values. In the Total row, you specify the summary function that the query applies.

➤ **To create a crosstab query by using the Crosstab Query wizard**

1. On the **Create** tab, in the **Queries** group, click **Query** Wizard.
2. In the **New Query** dialog box, select **Crosstab Query Wizard**, and then click **OK**.
3. On the wizard's first page, select the table or query on which to base the crosstab query, and then click **Next**.
4. Specify the field or fields (up to three fields) you want to use as row headings, and then click **Next**.
5. Select the field you want to use for the column headings, and then click **Next**.
6. If you chose a Date/Time field for the column heading in step 5, specify the interval for grouping date/time information in the column headings, and then click **Next**.
7. Select the field whose value you want to summarize and the function you want to apply, and then click **Next**.
8. Enter a name for the query, and then click **Finish**.

➤ **To create a crosstab query in Design view**

1. On the **Create** tab, in the **Queries** group, click **Query Design**.
2. In the **Show Table** dialog box, select the tables or queries you want to use in the query. Click **Add** to add the tables to the **Query Designer**, and then click **Close**.
3. From the table field lists, drag the fields you want to include in the query to the **Field** row in the query design grid. (You can also select fields from the list Access displays when you click in the **Field** row in the query design grid.)
4. Define any selection criteria for the query in the **Criteria** row.
5. In the **Query Type** group, click **Crosstab**.
6. In the **Crosstab** row, specify the field or fields you want to use for row headings, column headings, and the query's values.
7. In the **Total** row for the value field, select the summary function you want to apply.
8. In the **Results** group, click **Run** to display the query's results.

Union, pass-through, and data definition queries

The Query Type group also includes options for creating union, pass-through, and data definition queries. You need to define these types of queries by using the Structured Query Language (SQL). You can find more information about SQL queries by reading the Access Help topic "Introduction to Access SQL."

Managing multiple tables and joins

As you saw in examples earlier in this chapter, you use the Show Table dialog box to select multiple tables and other queries to include as a query's record source. To display the Show Table dialog box, you need to open a query in Design view.

A *join* is a link between two related tables in a query. To retrieve the records you need in a query, you use either an *inner join* or an *outer join*. The default join is an inner join. With an *inner join*, a query returns only records with matching rows in both tables. For example, a query that joins a projects table and a tasks table doesn't return records for projects that don't yet have any tasks assigned. This query also doesn't return records for tasks that aren't assigned to a specific project. By using an *outer join* in this query, you could retrieve the set of matching records (projects and their assigned tasks) in addition to projects without tasks (all projects) or tasks without projects (all tasks).

Whenever you have relationships defined between two tables, Access automatically joins the tables by using the fields in the defined relationships. Access also includes an option named Enable AutoJoin (which appears on the Object Designers page in the Access Options dialog box). This option is enabled by default, so when you create a query that includes tables that aren't directly related, Access tries to link the tables for you by examining the primary key fields for each table and then looking for a field with the same name and data type in one of the other tables in the query. If Access doesn't find a match, you can link the tables by selecting the linking field in one table and then dragging it to the field you want to link to in the second table. By joining the tables in this way, you link them for the purposes of designing and running the query. You don't create a permanent relationship that you can view and edit in the Relationships window.

See Also For more information about table relationships, see section 1.2, "Manage relationships and keys."

You can create a "left" outer join or a "right" outer join to retrieve all the records from one of the tables. *Left* and *right* refer to how the tables are identified in the Join Properties dialog box, which you open by right-clicking the line linking two tables in the Query Designer and then clicking Join Properties. To use an outer join to return all records from one table and matching records from another, click option 2 or 3, depending on which table's records you want to view.

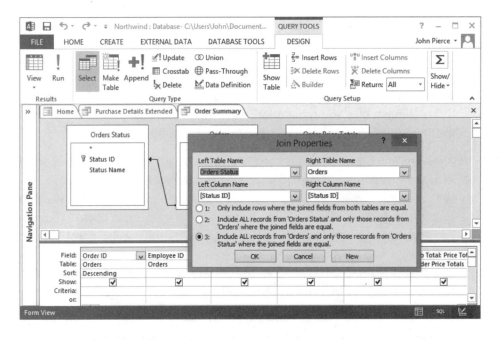

> **Tip** You can also specify the join type that related tables use when you have the Relationships window open. Click the relationship line for the tables you want to work with, and then click Edit Relationships in the Tools group on the Relationship Tools Design tool tab. Click Join Type in the Edit Relationships dialog box, and then click the option for the type of join you want to use.

➤ **To set up an outer join for tables in a query**

1. In the **Query Designer**, right-click the line linking the tables, and then click **Join Properties**.

2. In the **Join Properties** dialog box, click the option for the outer join you want to use.

Practice tasks

The practice file for these tasks is located in the MOSAccess2013\Objective3 practice file folder. You can save the results of the tasks in the same folder.

- Open the *Marketing_3* database.

- Use the Simple Query wizard to create a detail query that contains all the fields in the *CampaignExpenses* table. In the wizard, choose the option to view information so that you can examine the query's results.

- Open the *CampaignExpenses* query in Design view. Define criteria in the *AmountSpent* field to view only records for which the value of this field is greater than 500.

- Using the Query Designer, create a query based on the *MarketingCampaigns* table. Add the fields *CampaignID*, *Country*, and *CampaignBudget*. Create an update query to increase campaign budgets by 5 percent.

- Create a select query based on the *CampaignExpenses*, *CampaignExpense-Types*, and *MarketingCampaigns* tables. Add the *CampaignID* and *Country* fields from the *MarketingCampaign* table, the *ExpenseType* field from the *CampaignExpenseTypes* table, and the *AmountSpent* field from the *Campaign-Expenses* table. Run the query to display the records returned by the select query. Now convert this query to a crosstab query. Use the *AmountSpent* field as the value field. Try using the *Country* and *ExpenseType* fields as the row headings and column headings fields to display different views of the data. Also select different functions in the Total row for the *AmountSpent* field to obtain different views of the data.

- In the Navigation pane, open the *Tasks* query in Design view.
- Display the Show Table dialog box, and add the *MarketingCampaigns* table to the query.
- From the *MarketingCampaigns* table, add the *Country* field to the query, and then run the query to display the results.
- Display the Show Table dialog box again, and add the *Employees* table to the query. Remove the *MarketingCampaigns* table from the Query Designer.
- Link the *Tasks* and the *Employees* table by using the *EmployeeID* and *AssignedTo* fields.
- Add the *AssignedTo* field to the query, and then run the query to review the results. Use the Join Properties dialog box to create an outer join that shows all the records from the *Tasks* table. Run the query again to view how the outer join changes the query's results.

3.2 Modify queries

After you set up a query, you can modify it by changing or rearranging the fields, show-ing and hiding query fields, and sorting the query's results. You can also format the fields in a query. This section examines some of the ways you can modify a query.

> **Tip** You can rename a query by right-clicking the query in the Navigation pane and then clicking Rename. Renaming a query can affect database objects that use the query as a record source. Access provides options for managing objects that you rename. For more information, see section 2.2, "Format tables."

Changing the fields in a query

With a query open in Design view, you can add, remove, and rearrange the query's fields in several ways. To add fields, you can do the following:

- Drag additional fields from the field lists displayed in the top pane to a blank row in the query design grid.
- Insert a field between two other fields by dragging it to the column in the query design grid where you want to place the field. Access moves the other fields in the query to the right.

- Add a field by selecting it from the list in the Field row in the query design grid.
- Click Show Table in the Query Setup group to open the Show Table dialog box, and then select another table or query to include in the query's record source.

To remove a field, click the top of the field's column in the design grid, and then press Delete or click Delete Columns in the Query Setup group. You cannot use the Undo command to reverse this action.

The Query Setup group also contains options for inserting and deleting rows (when you need to define additional criteria, for example) and for opening the Expression Builder.

> **See Also** For more information about the Expression Builder, see the "Getting help from the Expression Builder" sidebar in section 3.3, "Utilize calculated fields and grouping with queries."

If you want to change the order of the fields in the grid, click in the top of the column in the design grid (hold down the Shift key and click to select more than one adjacent column), and then drag the field or fields to the new position. Access displays a black bar to indicate the new position.

➤ **To add, remove, and rearrange fields in a query**

1. In the Navigation pane, right-click the query, and then click **Design View**.
2. To insert a field, in the field list in the top pane of the **Query Designer**, select the field, and then drag the field to the query design grid.
3. To delete a field, click in the top of the field's column, and then press **Delete**.
4. To change the order of the fields, click the top of the column for the field you want to move (hold down the **Shift** key to select more than one column), and then drag the column or columns to the new location.

Showing and hiding query fields

By default, the check box in the Show row for each field in a query is selected. This means that the values in each field are displayed in the query's results. By clearing this check box for a field, you remove that field's values from the query's result without removing the field from the query.

The capability to hide a field is helpful when you want to use a field to define selection criteria or to sort a query but don't want to show the field in the query's results. Fields you use this way are essential to defining the query, but their values don't need to be shown in the query's results. You might add an ID field or a date field to a query for these purposes. For the ID field, you might specify a particular customer's ID. You could use the date field to sort records to display orders sequentially since the start of your fiscal year. The purpose of these fields is to tailor the query. Any reporting or analysis doesn't require that the query include the values that these fields provide.

➤ **To show and hide query fields**

1. In the Navigation pane, right-click the query, and then click **Design View**.
2. In the query design grid, clear the **Show** check box for any fields you want to hide.
3. Select the **Show** check box to display a field in the results.

Specifying the sort order for queries

You use the Sort row in the query design grid to specify how Access sorts the records returned by a query. You can sort by a single field or by more than one field. When you specify a sort order for more than one field, Access sorts records according to the order in which the fields appear left to right in the query design grid.

> **Tip** If you add all the fields from a table or query to the query design grid by dragging the asterisk, you cannot use the Sort row to sort records.

If you want to sort by multiple fields in a particular sequence but also display one of these fields later in the order of the fields, add a second instance of the field, set the sort order for the field, and then clear the Show check box so that the second instance of the field doesn't appear in the query's results.

To specify a sort order, click in the Sort row for a field, and then select the sort order you want to apply. The sorting options are Ascending, Descending, and Not Sorted. Be sure to reposition fields as you want them to appear when you are sorting records by more than one field.

> **See Also** For more information about how to rearrange field order, see the "Changing the fields in a query" topic earlier in this section.

➤ **To use the Sort row in a query**

1. In the Navigation pane, right-click the query, and then choose **Design View**.

2. In the query design grid, click in the **Sort** row for the field you want to sort by, and then select **Ascending**, **Descending**, or **Not Sorted**.

3. To sort by more than one field, specify the sort order for the additional fields. In the query design grid, arrange the fields from left to right in the order you want Access to use them to sort records.

Formatting fields in a query

At times, you might want to print the results of a query or save the results as a PDF file for distribution. To enhance the plain display of the results in the datasheet, you can apply text formatting from the Home tab. For example, you can display or hide gridlines, apply a background color to alternate rows, and apply font attributes such as bold or italic.

The text formatting you apply affects all the records in a query. You can't, for example, apply bold formatting to only one column of values in the query's datasheet. Even when you have a single column selected and click Bold in the Text Formatting group, the bold formatting is applied throughout the set of records. Perhaps the most useful text formatting tools are the options for adding or modifying alternate row colors and displaying gridlines to help distinguish the rows and columns of data.

In a query, you can use a field's Format property to display the values in that field differently from the way the field's format is specified in the table in which the field is defined. For example, a date field can be defined with the Short Date format in its table but displayed in the Long Date format in a query. You can also use a field's Caption property in a query to use a different label in the column heading. Setting the Format or Caption property for a field in a query does not define or change the property for the field in its table.

➤ **To set formatting properties for a field in a query**

1. Open the query in Design view.

2. On the **Query Tools Design** tool tab, in the **Show/Hide** group, click **Property Sheet**.

3. Click in the column for the field you want to format.

4. In the property sheet, enter or select a value for properties such as **Format** and **Caption**.

> **Practice tasks**
>
> The practice files for these tasks are located in the MOSAccess2013\Objective3 practice file folder. You can save the results of the tasks in the same folder.
>
> - Open the *Marketing_3* database.
> - Open the *TaskAssignments* query (*qryTasksAssignments*) in Design view, and make the following changes. Run the query after each change to check how the change affects the query's results.
>   - From the Tasks table, add the fields *TaskName*, *Description*, *Start Date*, and *Due Date*.
>   - Hide the field *Task ID*.
>   - Sort the query on the *Start Date* field.
>   - Create a caption for the *AssignedTo* field named *Current Assignments*.

3.3 Utilize calculated fields and grouping within queries

As described earlier in this chapter, queries let you select specific records and perform operations such as updating, deleting, or appending records. This section explains how queries can also summarize and group data. For example, you can use a query to show the average value in a field or to count the number of records that meet specific criteria. This chapter also provides examples of how to create a *calculated field*—a field whose data is derived from the values in other fields but not stored in the database itself. The end of this section explains more about expressions and about the array of operators you can use in Access to define query criteria.

Grouping and summarizing query records

When you set up and run a query in Design view, Access by default creates a detail query that returns each record that matches the query's fields and any criteria you define. For example, a query designed to show sales in each category by order date will display all the individual orders placed on a specific date. In a case like this, however, a more help-ful perspective on the data might be to display the total ordered for each category on a specific date instead of the amounts for each individual order.

To perform an operation such as this in a query, you use the Total row, which you display by clicking Totals in the Show/Hide group on the Query Tools Design tool tab.

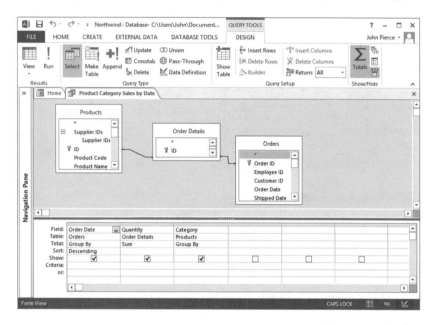

The Group By option is selected in the Total row when you insert the row. On its own, this option returns records that have unique values in each field in the query. However, you can use the Group By option together with a summary function to summarize data.

In this example, without the settings specified in the Total row, Access would display a record for each order when you run the query. After displaying the Total row and speci-fying the Sum function for the Quantity field, run the query again to display the records grouped by each order date and also the quantity ordered in each category that day.

Home	Product Category Sales by Date		Totals
Order Date	**SumOfQuan**	**Type**	
Friday, June 23, 2006	60	Dried Fruit & Nuts	
Thursday, June 8, 2006	40	Candy	
Wednesday, June 7, 2006	5	Beverages	
Monday, June 5, 2006	40	Candy	
Monday, June 5, 2006	40	Canned Fruit & Vegetables	
Monday, June 5, 2006	30	Condiments	
Monday, June 5, 2006	90	Jams, Preserves	
Monday, June 5, 2006	10	Soups	
Wednesday, May 24, 2006	40	Canned Meat	
Wednesday, May 24, 2006	35	Dried Fruit & Nuts	
Wednesday, May 24, 2006	20	Sauces	

Home	Product Category Sales by Date	
Order Date	**Quantity**	
Friday, June 23, 2006	30	Dried Fruit
Friday, June 23, 2006	30	Dried Fruit
Thursday, June 8, 2006	40	Candy
Wednesday, June 7, 2006	5	Beverages
Monday, June 5, 2006	40	Candy
Monday, June 5, 2006	40	Canned Fr
Monday, June 5, 2006	90	Jams, Preserves
Monday, June 5, 2006	10	Soups
Monday, June 5, 2006	30	Condiments
Wednesday, May 24, 2006	20	Sauces
Wednesday, May 24, 2006	40	Canned Meat
Wednesday, May 24, 2006	20	Dried Fruit & Nuts
Wednesday, May 24, 2006	15	Dried Fruit & Nuts

Individual orders in the same
category placed on the same day
are now summarized in this query

In addition to Sum, you can apply various other functions to the data in a summary query. The options in the Total row also include the following functions:

- **Avg** This calculates the average of the values in the field.

- **Min** This identifies the smallest value in the field.

- **Max** This identifies the highest value in the field.

- **Count** This counts the number of values in a field, but ignores Null (blank) values.

- **StDev** This shows you the standard deviation for the values in the field.

- **Var** This calculates the variance of the values in the field.

- **First** This returns the value for the field from the first row encountered in the group.

- **Last** This returns the value for the field from the last row encountered in the group.

- **Expression** Select this option when you want to create an expression in the Total row that uses one or more of the aggregate functions Access provides.

- **Where** Use this setting to apply a filter to the records in the query.

> **Tip** You can also use reports to summarize the data in a table or the results returned in a query. For more information about reports, see Chapter 5, "Create reports."

To display several summary values for a specific field at one time, add several instances of the field to the query and then choose a different summary function for each instance. For example, you could add three instances of the Quantity field to display the total quantity ordered in addition to the minimum and maximum quantities.

Creating custom field names

When you create a totals query, Access appends the name of the summary function to the field name and comes up with labels such as AvgOfQuantity. You can create your own labels in the Query Designer by entering the text you want to use in front of the field name in the Field row, followed by a colon. For example, instead of using AvgOfQuantity, you could enter *Average Quantity:* in front of the field name Quantity. Access uses this label when you display the query's results in Datasheet view.

You can apply criteria to a totals query to select specific records. For example, when you use the *Sum* function in the Total row, enter a value in the Criteria row to select values that are above or below a certain threshold—total quantities greater than 250, for example, **>250**. To apply a filter to a total query, select Where in the Total row, and then enter the criteria for the filter in the Criteria row.

➤ **To group records in a query**

1. In the Navigation pane, right-click the query, and then click **Design View**.
2. On the **Query Tools Design** tool tab, in the **Show/Hide** group, click **Totals**.
3. In the **Total** row, specify the settings you want for grouping fields.

➤ **To view summary data in a query**

1. In the Navigation pane, right-click the query, and then click **Design View**.
2. On the **Design** tool tab, in the **Show/Hide** group, click **Totals**.
3. In the **Total** row, select the summary function you want to apply to a field.
4. Use the **Criteria** row to define criteria you want to apply to the totals query.
5. To apply a filter to the query, select **Where** in the **Total** row, and then specify the filter criteria in the **Criteria** row.
6. On the **Design** tool tab, click **Run** to display the query's results.

Using calculated fields

You use expressions in many areas of Access—in validation rules, for example, and in the Control Source property on forms. Expressions contain several elements, including functions, operators, constants, and identifiers (which refer to the names of fields or tables, for example).

Expressions are used in queries to define criteria and can also be used to create a calculated field. For example, in a query that summarizes orders, you can use an expression to create a calculated field that shows the period of time between the order date and the date the order was shipped. This expression would look like the following:

[OrderDate]-[ShippedDate]

> **Tip** When you use an expression to create a calculated field, Access provides the default label *Expr1* (for the first expression in a query) as a column heading in the results datasheet. To rename the calculated field, enter the field name you want to use followed by a colon, and then enter the expression—for example:
>
> **Fulfillment Time:[OrderDate]-[ShippedDate]**

Identifiers, such as field names, are enclosed in square brackets. Here's another example of a calculated field, which uses the *IIf* and *Date* functions to define a conditional expression that notifies you if an invoice is past due.

IIf[Invoice Date]>Date()-30,"Past Due", "On Track"

The expression in this calculated field tests the value in the Invoice Date field, and if that date is later than 30 days from the current date (provided by the *Date* function), it displays *Past Due* in the calculated field. If the invoice date is earlier than 30 days from today, the calculated field displays *On Track*.

To create a calculated field in a query, open the query in Design view, and then click in the Field row in a blank column. (To insert a blank column between two fields already in the query, select the column at the right and then click Insert Columns in the Query Setup group.) You can enter the expression directly in the Field row or use the Zoom dialog box or the Expression Builder.

See Also For information about the Zoom dialog box, see the "Entering expressions in the Zoom dialog box" topic later in this section. For information about the Expression Builder, see the "Getting help from the Expression Builder" sidebar, also later in this section.

➤ **To create a calculated field**

1. Open the query in Design view.

2. In the **Query Designer**, click in the **Field** row in the column in which you want to insert the calculated field.

3. Enter the expression that performs the calculation.

   ○ To provide a custom label for the calculated field, enter the label you want to use before the expression, followed by a colon.

   ○ To open the **Zoom** dialog box to write the expression, press **Shift+F2**.

   ○ To open the Expression Builder for help writing the expression, click **Builder** in the **Query Setup** group.

Using operators in query criteria and expressions

Throughout this chapter are examples of different operators you can use in an expression that defines query criteria or a calculated field. The operators you can use include basic mathematical operators for addition (+), subtraction (–), multiplication (/), and division (*).

You can use the ampersand (&) to combine the values in two or more text fields. For example, the expression *[City] & ", " & [State/Province]* combines the City and State/Province fields in a single text string.

Access also provides logical operators (such as Or, And, and Not), and comparison operators such as < (less than), and > (greater than). Here are a few examples of how to use these operators in criteria expressions.

<Date()	Returns records with a date earlier than the current date
"Lee" or "Andersen"	Returns records with either Lee or Andersen as the value in the field
Not "Andersen"	Returns records except those with Andersen as the value in the field
Not <#4/1/2014#	Returns only records with a date later than 4/1/2014
<=50	Returns records with a value of 50 or less
<>"Beverages"	Returns records that do not equal Beverages in this field

Three other comparison operators are Like, In, and Between. The Like operator can be used to compare a field value to a text string. For example, the expression *Like "98###"* in a postal code field returns records in ZIP Codes that start with 98. You can use the In operator to find specific records. The expression *In "Las Vegas"* returns records with the value *Las Vegas* in the city field. Use the Between operator to locate the records within a range of dates (*Between #1/1/2013# And #1/30/2013#*) or a range of numbers (*Between 1200 And 1500*).

Entering expressions in the Zoom dialog box

When you need to write an expression to create a calculated field in a query or to define criteria, open the Zoom dialog box to give yourself some extra space in which to write the expression or to edit an expression that is already defined.

The Zoom dialog box provides a large text box in which you can compose an expression. Click the Font button in the Zoom dialog box to display the Font dialog box. You can then select a different font, font style, font size, and other attributes. Access doesn't display this formatting in the Query Designer, but the formatting might improve the readability of the expression while you are working with it in the Zoom dialog box.

➤ **To display the Zoom dialog box to write or review an expression**

1. In the query design grid, click in the cell where you want to write an expression—for example, a cell in the **Field** or **Criteria** row.

2. Press **Shift+F2**.

3. Click the **Font** button in the **Zoom** dialog box to format the text you enter there.

Getting help from the Expression Builder

When you want help creating an expression, you can use the Expression Builder. To open the Expression Builder in Design view, right-click in the Field or Criteria row and then click Build. You can also click Builder in the Query Setup group.

The Expression Builder has four panes. Create the expression in the top pane by entering the expression or by selecting options in the Expression Elements, Expression Categories, and Expression Values panes. The Expression Values pane is blank until you select an option other than the current object in the Expression Elements pane. (You can hide the three bottom panes by clicking Less. Click More to show them again.)

Build an expression by selecting items in the three bottom panes. In most cases, you build expressions from left to right. When you select an element in the Expression Elements list, the categories for that element appear in the Expression Categories pane. When you select a category, the Expression Builder lists the values related to that category in the Expression Values pane. Double-click an item in the Expression Values pane to add it to the expression.

For example, to create an expression that calculates the difference between the start date and the due date in the Tasks query, select the query name in the Expression Elements list, and then double-click Due Date in the Expression Categories list. In the Expression Elements list, select Operators; in the Expression Categories list, select Arithmetic, and then double-click the subtraction operator (–) in the Expression Value list. Now select the query again in the Expression Elements list, and then double-click Start Date in the Expression Categories list. The top pane displays the expression that you defined.

When you enter text in the Expression Builder's main pane, Access displays a list of items that match the characters you enter. You can choose a function name or a field name from this list to include it in the expression. As you continue entering characters, Access adjusts the list on the basis of each character you enter. Access also displays a description of the items in this list. When you select a function from the list or start entering a function's name, Access also provides information about the function's syntax, showing required and optional arguments.

Practice tasks

The practice file for these tasks is located in the MOSAccess2013\Objective3 practice file folder. You can save the results of the tasks in the same folder.

- Open the *Marketing_3* database, and then open the query *CampaignExpense-Summary* in Design view.

- Add the *Total* row, and summarize the *AmountSpent* field by using the Sum function, Min function, and Max function.

- From the *MarketingCampaigns* table, add the *CampaignBudget* field to the query, and then save the query.

- Create a calculated field that divides the *AmountSpent* field by the *Campaign-Budget* field. Create a label for the calculated field named Percent of Budget. Use the property sheet to apply the Percent format to this field. Hide the *CampaignBudget* field, and then run the query to display the results.

Objective review

Before finishing this chapter, be sure you have mastered the following skills:

3.1   Create a query

3.2   Modify queries

3.3   Utilize calculated fields and grouping within queries

4 Create forms

The skills tested in this section of the Microsoft Office Specialist exam for Microsoft Access 2013 relate to building forms. Specifically, the following objectives are associated with this set of skills:

4.1 Create a form

4.2 Set form controls

4.3 Format forms

Forms serve as a user interface for an Access database, simplifying how you navigate between objects, records, and features and helping you organize the work of inserting and updating data.

This chapter guides you in studying how to create a form by using commands on the Create tab and explains in detail how to work with form controls such as labels, text boxes, and list boxes. This chapter also describes control properties and how to move, arrange, and format controls. Finally, this chapter covers aspects of formatting a form, including how to set a form's tab order, modify a form's background, and sort the records displayed in a form.

> **Tip** Chapter 5, "Create reports," covers Access reports. Forms and reports have several characteristics in common. When you create and modify reports, you apply many of the same skills that are covered in this chapter.

> **Practice Files** To complete the practice tasks in this chapter, you need the practice files contained in the MOSAccess2013\Objective4 practice file folder. For more information, see "Download the practice files" in this book's Introduction.

4.1 Create a form

Access can create a fully functioning form in a single step, or you can start with a blank form and then place and define each element of a form yourself. Access also provides tools for creating forms that use a specific form layout, including a navigation form.

> **See Also** For more information about creating a navigation form, see section 1.3, "Navigate through databases." For more information about adding forms to a database by using application parts, see section 1.1, "Create new databases."

You work with several elements in forms. Forms use *controls* to display data (a text box or a list box, for example), to identify information (label controls), to aid navigation (hyperlinks and button controls), and to organize and emphasize aspects of a form's layout (line and rectangle controls). Both a form and its controls use *properties* to define their data source and to define their size and position, their format, and other aspects of their appearance and behavior.

Most of a form's data controls are displayed in the form's Detail section. A form also includes a Header section for titles, logos, and labels, and a Footer section that you can use to display calculated fields, for example.

When you use a wizard to create a form, the wizard sets most properties to default values. You can adjust these settings by using the form's property sheet and by using tools on three form-related tabs on the ribbon: the Design tab, the Arrange tab, and the Format tab.

Access displays these tabs when you create or modify a form in Layout view or Design view. In Layout view, Access displays the form's data while you work on the form, which lets you resize the form's controls (a text box, for example) to fit the data. Layout view also provides additional visual guidance about how the final form will appear. For example, Access displays formatting and color schemes as you design the form. In Design view, live data isn't displayed as you create the form, but Design view often provides a clearer definition of the form's structure, because each section of a form—the Header, Detail, and Footer sections—is labeled. Design view also offers more types of form controls and access to form properties (such as the Default View property) that aren't available in Layout view.

> **Tip** You can open a form in a specific view by right-clicking the form in the Navigation pane and then selecting the view you want. You can also click View in the Views group (on the Design tab) to switch between views, or change views by clicking the View buttons at the lower-right corner of the Access window.

Building forms by using the Form wizard

The fastest way to create a form is to select a table or a query in the Navigation pane and then click Form in the Forms group on the Create tab. Access creates a form that includes all the fields in the table or query (which serves as the form's record source) and displays the form in Layout view.

You can use a form you create by using the Form command to work with a single record at a time. Display the form in Form view, or start modifying the form in Layout view or Design view to add other controls, change formatting, and define features.

You can build a form almost as quickly—and gain options for selecting fields and a form layout—by using the Form wizard. The Form wizard uses the table or query selected in the Navigation pane as the default choice for the form's record source. On the wizard's first page, you can choose a different object or add fields from additional tables or queries.

The Form wizard offers four layout options: Columnar, Tabular, Datasheet, and Justified. When you select a layout, the wizard shows a preview of how the form will appear.

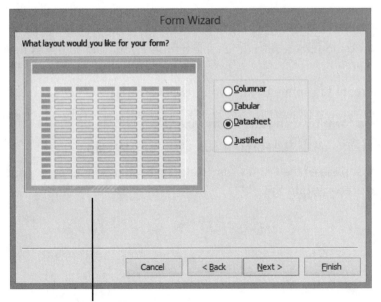

The Form wizard displays a preview for each layout option

On the wizard's final page, Access assigns a default name to the form and prompts you to either open the form to work with data or open the form in Design view to modify it.

See Also For information about working in Design view, see the "Creating forms in Design view" topic later in this section, and the "Sizing and ordering controls in Design view" topic in section 4.2, "Set form controls."

Creating a main form and a subform

Subforms let you work with records from another table or query within a main form. To create a main form and subform by using the Form wizard, choose the table or query for the main form and then add the fields you want to use. While still on the wizard's first page, select the table or query on which to base the subform, and then add the fields you want to include in the subform. On the next page, you choose between creating a form with a subform and creating two linked forms. Choose the option to create a subform, click Next, and then complete the steps in the wizard. For more information, see the "Creating subforms" topic later in this section.

➤ **To create a quick form**

1. In the Navigation pane, select the table or query you want to use as the form's record source.

2. On the **Create** tab, in the **Forms** group, click **Form**.

➤ **To create a form by using the Form wizard**

1. On the **Create** tab, in the **Forms** group, click **Form Wizard**.

2. On the first page of the **Form** wizard, select the table or query you want to use as the form's record source.

3. Move the fields you want to include on the form from the **Available Fields** list to the **Selected Fields** list, and then click **Next**.

4. Choose a layout for the form. Use the previews that the wizard displays when you select a layout option to view the form's general appearance.

5. Enter a name for the form (or accept the default name), and then specify whether you want to open the form to view and update data, or open the form in Design view to modify the form. Click **Finish** to create the form.

Creating forms in Layout view

If you want to build a form from scratch in Layout view, click Blank Form in the Forms group on the Create tab. Access displays a form window and the field list.

> **Tip** Double-click the field list's title bar to dock the list at the right side of the Access window.

In the field list, if the database's tables aren't listed, click Show All Tables. Click the plus sign (+) beside the table you want to use as the form's record source to display a list of the table's fields. You can then drag a field from the field list (or double-click the field) to place it on the form. After you add a field from a specific table to the form, Access updates the field list, dividing it into three areas:

- **Fields Available For This View** Shows the fields from the table you selected as the record source.

- **Fields Available In Related Tables** Lists the tables related to the table that's serving as the record source.

- **Fields Available In Other Tables** Lists the other tables in the database. (If all the tables in the database are related to the table you are using, Access does not display this group.)

Click this link to show only
the fields on the form

Click here to open a
table in Datasheet view

> **See Also** For more information about creating table relationships, see section 1.2,
> "Manage relationships and keys."

By default, the fields you add to a form in Layout view are stacked in columns. Each
field's label appears in a column on the left, and the field's input control (a text box or
a list box, for example) appears on the right. When you drag a field from the field list to
the form, Access displays an orange bar at the bottom of the stack; drag up to insert the
field between fields already on the form. To add a column, right-click a control on the
form, click Insert, and then click Insert Left or Insert Right. To insert a row, right-click a
control, click Insert, and then click Insert Above or Insert Below.

> **See Also** For more information about arranging fields on a form in Layout view, see the
> "Working with control layouts in Layout view" topic in section 4.2, "Set form controls."

The field list includes links that you can use to change which fields it displays and to work with data. Click Show Only Fields In The Current Record Source at the top of the field list to display only those fields you have added to the form. Click Edit Table (which appears to the right of a table's name) to open a table in Datasheet view, where you can view, insert, or update data while you are designing the form.

Use the Property Sheet command in the Tools group on the Form Layout Tools Design tool tab to view values for the form's properties and properties for the controls included on the form. (When you display the property sheet, Access hides the field list. Click Add Existing Fields in the Tools group to open the field list again.)

To view the form's Record Source property, for example, click Property Sheet, and then select Form in the Selection Type list at the top of the property sheet. On the property sheet's Data tab, click in the Record Source box, and then press Shift+F2 to open the Zoom dialog box. Access uses a SELECT statement (an element of the Structured Query Language, or *SQL*) to identify the table and the fields you've added to the form. For example, the following SELECT statement identifies four fields in the table named *MarketingCampaigns*.

```
SELECT MarketingCampaigns.Country, MarketingCampaigns.LaunchDate,
MarketingCampaigns.EndDate, MarketingCampaigns.Audience FROM MarketingCampaigns
```

> **See Also** For more information about control properties, see the "Working with control properties" topic in section 4.2, "Set form controls."

When you add a field to a form, Access uses the field's data type to determine which type of form control to associate with the field. In many cases (for text and number fields, for example), Access creates a text box control and an associated label. For lookup fields, Access creates a combo box control, and for Yes/No fields, Access inserts a check box control. You can add other types of controls—a command button, for example, or a label control—by using the options in the Controls group on the Design tool tab. Select the type of control you want to add, and then click in the form where you want the control to appear.

You can use the commands in the Header/Footer group on the Design tool tab to add a title, logo, or date and time to a form. The Title command adds a label you can update to name the form. Click Logo to open the Insert Picture dialog box, where you can select an image file for a logo you want to include. The Date And Time command opens a dialog box in which you can select the date and time format you want to display on the form.

➤ **To create a form in Layout view**

1. On the **Create** tab, in the **Forms** group, click **Blank Form**.

2. In the field list, if no tables are shown, click **Show All Tables**, and then click the plus (+) sign beside the table you want to use as the form's record source. If the field list is not displayed, click **Add Existing Fields** on the **Form Layout Tools Design** tool tab.

3. In the field list, drag the fields you want to include on the form and place them in the form window. You can align and reposition fields after you place them.

4. To add a logo, title, or date and time to the form, use the commands in the **Header/Footer** group on the **Design** tool tab.

5. On the **Design** tool tab, click **Property Sheet**.

6. In the property sheet, specify properties for the form and the form's controls.

Creating forms in Design view

The Form Design command in the Create tab's Forms group opens a blank form window in Design view. The tools and methods you use to create a form in Design view are similar to those you work with in Layout view. On the Form Design Tools Design tool tab, click Add Existing Fields in the Tools group to open the field list. You can then expand the list of fields for the table you want to use as the form's record source and drag fields to place them on the form. When you add the first field to the form, Access updates the fields displayed in the field list as it does in Layout view.

> **See Also** For more information about adding fields to a form, see the "Creating forms in Layout view" topic earlier in this chapter.

Select Form, a form section, or a control from
this list to view the properties for an object

As you add fields to the form, Access starts defining the form's Record Source property. (You can find an example of the expression Access uses to create a form's record source in the previous section.) To view or modify the Record Source and other properties, click Property Sheet in the Tools group on the Design tool tab. From the Selection Type list, select the form, control, or form section (Detail, for example) whose properties you want to update or view.

To align and position fields when you work in Design view, use the grid marks and the ruler. Access highlights the ruler when you drag a control and shows the control's position relative to other controls. By right-clicking a control, you can work with the options on the Align, Size, and Position menus to adjust the layout of the form. For example, to align a group of labels, select the group by holding down the Ctrl key and clicking each label, right-click the selection, point to Align, and then click the Left or Right option.

> **See Also** For more information about arranging controls, see the "Sizing and ordering controls in Design view" topic in section 4.2, "Set form controls."

When you first create a form in Design view, the form contains only the Detail section. You locate most of the form's controls in its Detail section, but a form can also include a Header and Footer section. Use the Header section to display the form's title, to include a logo, or to show the date and time, for example. You might use the Footer section to show a Totals field that is calculated from the values of other fields on the form.

To insert the Header and Footer sections, right-click in the Detail section, and then click Form Header/Footer. You can also use the commands in the Header/Footer group on the Design tool tab to add the Header and Footer sections and insert a form element. The Title command adds a label to the Header section. Click Logo to open the Insert Picture dialog box, in which you can select the image file for a logo you want to include. The Date And Time command opens a dialog box that you can use to select a format in which to display the date and time. Access adds the date, time, or both to the form's Header section.

To add a control to the form, click the type of control you want to add in the Controls group, and then click on the form where you want to place the control. For text box, combo box, and list box controls, Access displays a wizard by default that helps you set up the properties and functionality of the control.

> **See Also** For more information about adding form controls and setting control properties, see the "Adding, moving, and deleting form controls" topic in section 4.2, "Set form controls."

➤ **To create a form in Design view**

1. On the **Create** tab, in the **Forms** group, click **Form Design**.

2. To display the field list, click **Add Existing Fields** in the **Tools** group on the **Form Design Tools Design** tool tab.

3. In the field list, click **Show All Tables** (if no tables are shown), and then click the plus (+) sign beside the table you want to use as the form's record source.

4. In the field list, drag the fields you want to include on the form and place them in the form window. You can align and reposition fields after you place them.

5. To add a logo, title, or date and time to the form, use the commands in the **Header/Footer** group.

6. On the **Design** tool tab, click **Property Sheet**.

7. In the property sheet, specify properties for the form and the form's controls.

Creating subforms

By creating a subform that you display within a main form, you can view data from related tables—for example, you can use a subform to display detailed budget records when the summary budget amount is displayed on the main form. You can define a main form and a subform when you use the Form wizard, but if you want to add a subform to a form you have already created, you can use the SubForm wizard, which appears when you insert a subform/subreport control on a form.

> **Tip** To use the SubForm wizard, be sure the Use Controls Wizard option is selected in the Controls group on the Form Design Tools Design tool tab (or Form Layout Tools Design tool tab). Click the subform/subreport control, and then click the form to run the wizard.

You can base a subform on a table, query, or form you've already defined. If you click the option Use An Existing Form, select the form in the list, click Next, enter a name for the subform, and then click Finish. When you select the Use Existing Tables And Queries option, the wizard displays a page on which you choose fields from one or more tables to include on the subform. On the wizard's next page, you define which field links the subform and the main form. If the table or query you selected has a relationship to the main form's record source, Access shows a list of fields you can choose from. If Access cannot determine the linking fields, it selects the Define My Own option on this page. You then need to select the linking fields you want to use.

If you want to fine-tune the work the wizard performed, select the subform control, open the property sheet, and then adjust the Height and Width properties, for example, reposition the control by setting the Top and Left properties, or enter a message in the Status Bar Text property (on the property sheet's Other tab) to describe the purpose of the subform.

Setting form properties

A form and its sections (Detail, Header, and Footer) have numerous properties you can set and modify in the property sheet. With the property sheet open, select Detail, Form Header, or Form Footer from the Selection Type list to view and set properties for that section. Select Form to work with the properties for the form itself.

For a form, you might work with one or more of the following properties on the property sheet's Format tab.

- **Default View** Use the Default View property to specify the view in which Access opens the form when you double-click the form in the Navigation pane or click Form View on the View menu. The options are Datasheet, Single Form (which displays a single record on the form), and Continuous Forms (which displays multiple records).

- **Allow Form View, Allow Datasheet View, Allow Layout View** Use these properties to control the views in which you can display the form.

- **Navigation Buttons, Navigation Caption, Scroll Bars, Record Selectors** Set the Navigation buttons property to No if the record navigation buttons aren't required on the form. If you do show the navigation buttons, you can enter text in the Navigation Caption property to replace the default caption *Record*. The Scroll Bars property gives you options for showing only the vertical scroll bar, only the horizontal scroll bar, both, or neither. The Record Selectors property controls whether the record selector is displayed on the form.

- **Close Button, Min Max Buttons** Set these properties to Yes or No depending on whether you want the form to include the Close, Minimize, or Maximize buttons in the upper-right corner of the form.

On the property sheet's Data tab, you can view and set properties that affect how a user works with the form's data.

- **Data Entry** Set this property to Yes (the default setting is No) if you want Access to display a blank record when you open the form.

- **Allow Additions, Allow Deletions, Allow Edits** These properties control whether a user can use this form to insert records, delete records, and change the values in form controls.

- **Allow Filters** Set this property to No if you don't want users to be able to filter the records shown in this form.

Modifying existing forms

If you create a database by using one of the templates Access provides or add forms to a database by using application parts, you can follow the steps outlined in this chapter to modify the forms the templates provide. Use the Tools group on the Form Design Tools Design tool tab (or Form Layout Tools Design tool tab) to display the field list and the property sheet. For more detailed information about form controls and control properties, see the "Adding, moving, and deleting form controls" topic in section 4.2, "Set form controls." You should review this topic to learn how to use the field list and the property sheet to add fields to a form, move and position controls, and set control properties.

Saving and deleting forms

Any form you create by using one of the wizards is automatically saved by Access. When you design a form from scratch in Layout view or Design view, Access assigns a default name to the form (*Form1*, for example). To name and save the form, click Save on the Quick Access Toolbar or use the Save command in the Backstage view.

You can use options on the Save As page in the Backstage view to create a copy of a form as a new database object (click Save Object As) or as a PDF or an XPS file. The Save Object As command can be helpful if you want to experiment with a form that's already designed (by adding additional controls or changing formats, for example) and don't want to risk inadvertent changes to the original form.

To delete a form from a database, right-click the form in the Navigation pane, and then click Delete.

➤ **To save a form**

1. On the **Quick Access Toolbar**, click **Save**.

2. In the **Save As** dialog box, enter a name for the form, and then click **OK**.

➤ **To delete a form**

→ In the Navigation pane, right-click the form, and then click **Delete**.

Creating views in an Access web app

In an Access web app, views serve the purpose of forms in a desktop database. Access provides fewer tools for designing and formatting a view, but the steps you take to create a view are comparable to those required to create a form.

To work with the built-in views or create a view of your own, open an Access web app for customization in Access. (If you open the web app in your browser, click the Settings button at the right side of the browser window, and then click Customize In Access.) On the Home tab, click View, which displays a window where you name the view, specify the view type, and select the record source. You can choose one of four options for the view type: List Details, Datasheet, Summary, or Blank. List Details and Datasheet are the standard views that Access provides for each table provided in a web app template. Both of these view types include all the fields in the record source by default. In a summary view, you can group and summarize data by different values. You use the Blank option to add specific fields and controls to a view.

After Access creates the view, click Edit to add fields and controls to the view. The number and types of controls you can add depend on the type of view you create. For example, the Datasheet view is compatible with only six controls—label, text box, combo box, check box, auto-complete, and multiline text box. When you start with a blank view, you can use these and several other controls, including image and hyperlink controls. Use the field list to add fields from the view's record source and from other tables in the web app. You can apply font formatting to a control you add to a view, define a tooltip, and set properties such as Caption and Visible.

Use the field list
to build a view

Click the Format button to display
a set of control properties

➤ **To create a view in an Access web app**

1. Open the web app in Access.

2. On the **Home** tab, click **View**.

3. In the **Add New View** dialog box, enter the name of the view, select the view type, and then specify the record source.

4. Click **Add New View**.

5. Click **Edit**.

6. Use the field list and the options on the **View Design** tool tab to build and format the view.

Practice tasks

The practice files for these tasks are located in the MOSAccess2013\Objective4 practice file folder. You can save the results of the tasks in the same folder.

- Open the *Marketing_4* database.

- Use the Form command to create a form for the *Tasks* table.

- In the property sheet, display the properties for the form.

- Change the settings for some of the properties described in this section (such as those related to form navigation, scroll bars, and form views), and then display the form in Form view to check the effects of these changes.

- Use the Form wizard to create a form based on the *CampaignInfo* query (*qryCampaignInfo*). Add all the fields to the form. Notice that the wizard prompts you to create a subform.

- Complete the wizard, and then open the form in Design view.

- Use the Date And Time command to add the date to the form's header.

- You can delete these test forms when you complete these exercises.

4.2 Set form controls

This section explains more about working with form controls. It describes how to add, move, and delete controls and the properties you can use to define a control's format and behavior. This section also covers more about working with controls in Layout and Design view and the options you have for arranging and formatting controls from the ribbon. In addition, it describes how to modify data sources for forms and controls and how to work with labels.

Adding, moving, and deleting form controls

The Controls group on the Form Design Tools Design tool tab (or Form Layout Tools Design tool tab) displays an icon for each type of control you can use on a form. (A ScreenTip identifies each type of control.) Open a form in Layout view or Design view, click a control icon (for a text box, command button, or check box, for example), and then click in the form where you want the control to appear.

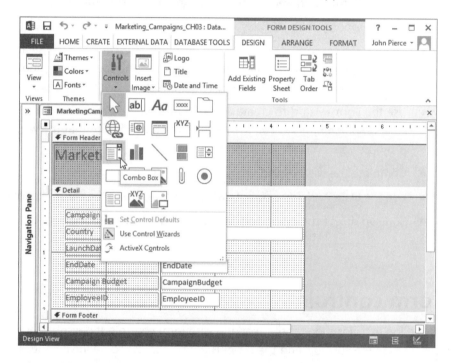

After adding a control, you can drag it to change and fine-tune its position. You can also select a control and then use the arrow keys to move it up, down, left, or right. Use the arrow keys to move a control in smaller increments than dragging often affords. Drag a control's border to move the control and its label together. Point to the larger gray handle in a control's upper-left corner to move a label or a control independently. To move a control to a precise position, open the property sheet and specify coordinates for the Top and Left properties. The settings for the Top and Left properties position a control relative to the upper-left corner of the form.

To drag a label or a text box independently,
use the handle in the upper-left corner of the control

To delete a control, right-click the control, and then click Delete. If a label is associated
with a control you delete, Access also deletes the label.

➤ To add a control to a form

1. Open the form in Design view or Layout view.
2. On the **Form Design Tools Design** tool tab (or **Form Layout Tools Design** tool tab),
   in the **Controls** group, click the icon for the type of control you want to add. Use
   the ScreenTips that Access displays to identify the control.
3. Click in the form where you want to place the control.
4. If prompted by Access, use the control wizard to set up the control.

➤ To move and position controls

→ Select the control, and then drag the control or use the arrow keys to position the
   control.

➤ To delete a control

→ Right-click the control, and then click **Delete**.

Using control wizards

By default, Access enables the option Use Control Wizards (which you can select or clear in the Controls group) and displays a wizard when you insert a button, combo box, or list box on a form. The following summarizes the steps you follow when you work with particular wizards.

- **Command Button wizard** On the wizard's first page, select a category, and then select an action for the button to perform. In the Record Navigation category, for example, you can specify that the button goes to the next or previous record or finds a specific record. In the Form Operations category, the actions include Close Form, Print A Form, and Refresh Form Data, among others. You can choose an option to add a picture or a text label for a button. In the last step, you provide a name for the button. Use this name to refer to the button in expressions or macros.

- **Combo Box wizard and List Box wizard** In these wizards, you first specify whether the list items come from a table or a query or from a list that you define. Work through the wizard to select the table and fields, or enter the values in the list. Before you complete the steps in the wizard, you need to specify whether Access should remember the value selected in the list (you might use this value in an expression) or should save the value in a particular field.

Working with control properties

To display the property sheet, open a form in Design view or Layout view, and then click Property Sheet on the Form Design Tools Design tool tab (or the Form Layout Tools Design tool tab). The property sheet is arranged in five tabs: Format, Data, Event, Other, and All. Form controls share some properties (such as the Name property), and each type of control also has specific properties related to its type. The following list describes some of the properties you often work with.

- The Format tab includes properties such as Caption, Height, Width, Text Align, and Visible. Use a control's Visible property to show or hide the control under conditions you define.

- The Data tab includes the Control Source property—the property that binds a control to data in a specific field or uses an expression to derive the control's data. Not all types of controls have a Control Source property. Bound controls (controls that are linked to a field) include text boxes, option groups (which contain option buttons or check boxes), combo boxes and list boxes, charts, and subforms and subreports. Unbound controls include labels, command and toggle buttons, tab controls, hyperlinks, the web browser control, lines, and images. The Data tab also includes properties such as Default Value, Validation Rule, and Validation Text.

> **See Also** For more information about field validation rules and the Default Value property, see section 2.4, "Create and modify fields."

- The Event tab lists properties such as On Click, Before Update, On Enter, and On Exit. You can associate a macro or a subprocedure written in Microsoft Visual Basic for Applications (VBA) with an event property to automate the operations of a form.

- The Other tab contains the Name property (in addition to other properties). You use the Name property to refer to a control in VBA code and in an expression. The Name property is not the same as the Caption property, which controls the display text associated with a control. Access creates a default value for the Name property (such as Text10 or List6) when you add a control. Update the Name property to make a control's purpose or relationship to a field clearer. You can use the ControlTip Text property on the Other tab to define the text for a ScreenTip that appears when you point to the control with your mouse.

- The All tab displays all properties associated with a control.

The following list describes the purpose of each form control and identifies additional control properties related to the type of control.

- **Text box** Displays text fields and general number and currency fields. In addition to using the Width and Height properties to specify the size of a text box control, you can format a text box by setting properties such as Back Color, Border Style, Border Width, Font Name, and Font Size. For a field that uses the Long Text data type, set the Scroll Bars property to Vertical to more easily review the text that's displayed.

- **Label** Identifies fields and controls on the form. Formatting properties for labels include Font Name, Font Size, Font Weight and Border Style, Border Width, and Border Color. You can use the Special Effect property to give the label a sunken or raised look.

- **Button** Used to perform an action such as opening another form, navigating to records, or running macros or VBA code. You can set a variety of formatting properties for buttons. For example, you can add a picture to a button. You can use the Hover Color and Pressed Color properties to specify the color of the button and its text when you point to or press the button.

- **Tab** Provides a set of pages on which you can organize related data. In a database that tracks projects, for example, you could use one page of a tab control for schedule information, a second for budget fields, and a third for displaying data about task assignments. You can set properties for the tab control in general and for each page (tab). You can add text boxes, list boxes, buttons, and other types of controls to a page to define and interact with the data it displays.

- **Hyperlink** Links to a file, a webpage, or an email address. In a desktop database, you can also use a hyperlink to open another object in the database. When you add a hyperlink control to a form, Access displays the Insert Hyperlink dialog box. In the Link To list, select a category. If you select Existing File Or Web Page, you can use the Browse The Web or the Browse For File button to locate the page or file. Use the Address box to specify the URL or path, and enter the text you want to display on the form in the Text To Display box. For email addresses, you need to provide the address and the text for the message's Subject line.

- **Web browser** Displays a file or a webpage on a form. When you add a browser control to a form, Access opens the Insert Hyperlink dialog box with the Hyperlink Builder option selected. In the dialog box, enter the page URL or browse to the page you want to display. Access adds the URL to the Base URL box. For example, you could use *http://bing.com* as the base URL. When you enter */search?q=* in the Paths area and then define a parameter named *Term* with the value *Microsoft + Office* in the Parameters area, the control returns search results related to Microsoft Office. You can also use an expression to provide a value from a control on your form.

- **Navigation** Provides buttons that you can link to forms or reports.

> **See Also** For more information about using the navigation control, see section 1.3, "Navigate through databases."

- **Combo box** Lets users select an item from a list or specify a new item. You can restrict users from entering new items by setting the control's Limit To List property to Yes. You can format a combo box by setting font and border properties. A combo box's data properties include the Row Source property, which specifies the list's values, and Row Source Type, which indicates whether the list comes from fields in a table or a query or is defined by a value list that you create. Access provides a wizard that helps you set up a combo box.

- **List box** Displays a list of values from a table or a query or from a list that you define. As with a combo box, you use the Row Source and Row Source Type properties to set up the list.

- **Check box** Specifies yes/no or true/false choices. A check box has fewer formatting properties than other types of controls. Use the Control Source property to bind the control to a field.

- **Attachment** Bind this control to a field defined with the Attachment data type. Use the entries on the property sheet's Format tab to specify border styles, height, width, and any special effects.

- **Subform/subreport** Lets you embed another form or report within the form.

> **See Also** For more information about subforms, see the "Creating subforms" topic in section 4.1 "Create a form."

- **Image** Displays a logo or another type of image on a form.

- **Option group** Creates an option group that can contain check boxes, option buttons, or toggle buttons. When you bind an option group to a field, the value of that field can be determined by which option button or check box a user selects in the group. For example, you could bind an option group to the field ShipOptions and include option buttons for Express, Second Day, and Ground.

- **Option button** Captures yes/no or true/false information. You can add a set of option button controls to an option group to set the value for the field bound to the option group.

- **Page break** Inserts a page break between pages of a multipage form.

- **Chart** Inserts a chart on a form. Access displays the Chart wizard, which you use to select the fields whose data the chart displays, the type of chart, the chart's layout, and other properties.

- **Line** Adds a line to visually separate controls.

- **Toggle button** Captures yes/no information. When a toggle button is clicked (appears pressed in), its value is yes or true. When the button is not clicked, its value is false.

- **Rectangle** Adds a filled or empty rectangle to a form. You can enclose controls in a rectangle to help format the form.

- **Unbound object frame** Use for adding an object from another program to your form. The program needs to support object linking and embedding (OLE). You can add pictures, sounds, charts, slides, and worksheets, for example.

- **Bound object frame** Use for displaying and editing an OLE object field from the form's record source. You can display pictures and graphs on a form. For other types of objects, Access displays the icon representing the object's program.

➤ **To insert controls and set control properties**

1. In the Navigation pane, right-click the form, and then click **Design View** or **Layout View**.

2. On the **Form Design Tools Design** tool tab (or the **Form Layout Tools Design** tool tab), in the **Controls** group, click the control you want to add to the form.

3. Click in the form where you want to place the control. Depending on the type of control, Access displays a wizard or a dialog box, which you use to specify the information required to set up the control.

4. On the **Design** tool tab, in the **Tools** group, click **Property Sheet**.

5. In the property sheet, specify the values for the control properties you want to set.

Formatting form controls

By setting properties such as Back Color and Border Style in the property sheet, you can define or modify how a control appears. Options for formatting controls are also available on the ribbon, by working with commands on the Format tool tab that appears when a form is open in Layout view or Design view. For example, in the Font group on the Format tool tab, you can make changes to font properties for labels and other controls on the form.

> **Tip** The Font group includes the Format Painter button. Apply the font formatting you want to one control, click that control to select it, and then use the Format Painter to capture and apply those changes to other controls on the form.

To format a label, select it and then choose the font you want to use from the Font list. You can also change the font size and color or apply a background color to a control. Use the alignment buttons to position the text in the label as flush left, flush right, or centered.

In the Number group on the Format tool tab, you can apply a format to fields that use the Number, Currency, or Date/Time data type. For example, select a date field on a form, and then choose Medium Date, Long Date, Short Date, or another option from the Format list. The format you choose here affects how the date is displayed, but it doesn't change the date format specified for the field in table Design view.

In the Format tool tab's Control Formatting group, use the Shape Fill command to add a background color to a control. The Shape Outline command lets you modify the color and style of a control's borders. For a command button, you can use options on the Shape Effects menu to apply a shadow, a glow effect, or softened or beveled edges. Access enables the Change Shape command when you select a command button, tab control, or navigation button, for example. Use the options to display the button as an oval or another of the available shapes. For button controls, you can apply a set of formats by choosing an option in the gallery that appears when you click Quick Styles.

➤ To format form controls

1. Open the form in Layout view or Design view.
2. Click the **Form Design Tools Format** tool tab (or **Form Layouts Tools Design** tool tab).
3. In the **Selection** group, choose the control you want to format, or click **Select All**. (You can also click to select a control on the form.)
4. In the **Font** group, choose a new font, font size, or font color; apply bold, italic, or underline formatting; add a background fill color; and align the text.

5. For **Number**, **Currency**, and **Date/Time** fields, use the **Number** group to apply number, date/time, and currency formatting to the field.

6. In the **Control Formatting** group, do the following:

- ○ Use the **Quick Style** and **Change Shape** commands to format a button.
- ○ Use the **Shape Fill** command to add a background fill color to a control.
- ○ Use the **Shape Outline** command to apply line styles and colors to the control's borders.
- ○ Use the **Shape Effects** command to add a shadow or glow effect to a button control.

Modifying data sources

A form and the controls that it contains are tied to a data source. For a form, a *data source*—also referred to as a *record source*—can be based on a single table, multiple tables, or a query (which is itself based on one or more tables). The data source for a specific control is governed by the Control Source property. The Control Source property can be set to a specific field in the form's record source or to an expression. For example, you can add a text box to a form and enter an expression such as *=Sum([ExtendedPrice])* [Discount]* to add the values in the ExtendedPrice field, and then multiply that amount by the value of the Discount field, which produces the discounted amount of an order.

To modify the record source for a form, open the property sheet and then click the property sheet's Data tab. You can choose a different table or query by clicking in the Record Source box and then clicking the arrow to display a list of tables and queries in the database. You can also click the ellipsis button (...) in the Record Source box to open the Query Builder, which is similar to the Query Designer. In the Query Builder, click Show Table on the Query Tools Design tool tab to open the Show Table dialog box. You can then select other tables or queries to add to the form's record source. Use the Field list in the design grid to select the fields you want to include on the form. If a form is based on a query, the Query Builder displays the record source as a SQL statement that you can edit if you are familiar with SQL keywords and other elements. Close the Query Builder to return the form to Design view.

> **See Also** For more information about the Query Designer, see all sections in Chapter 3, "Create queries."

A form also has a Record Source Type property that you can set to one of three values to specify how users work with the form to insert and update data:

- **Dynaset** This is the default setting. When the Record Source Type property is set to Dynaset, you can edit bound controls based on a single table or on tables with a one-to-one relationship. For controls bound to fields based on tables with a one-to-many relationship, you cannot edit data from the linking field for the table on the "one" side of the relationship unless the Cascade Update option is set for the relationship between the tables.

- **Dynaset (Inconsistent Updates)** Specifying this setting makes all controls bound to a field editable.

- **Snapshot** Specify Snapshot to prevent updates to any of the fields displayed on a form.

To modify the Control Source property for a specific control, open the property sheet and display its Data tab. Click in the Control Source box, and then choose another field from the form's record source, or click the ellipsis to open the Expression Builder, which you can use to create an expression for a calculated control.

> **See Also** For more information about modifying data sources for forms and reports, see the "Modifying data sources" topic in section 5.2, "Set report controls." For more information about the Expression Builder, see section 3.3, "Utilize calculated fields and grouping within queries."

➤ To modify a form's data source

1. Open the form in Design view.

2. On the **Form Design Tools Design** tool tab, in the **Tools** group, click **Property Sheet** (if the property sheet is not displayed).

3. On the property sheet's **Data** tab, click in the **Record Source** property box.

4. Select a different table or query from the list in the property box.

   Or

   Click the ellipsis to open the Query Builder, use the Query Builder to modify the fields in the form's record source, and then close the Query Builder.

5. Set the **Record Source Type** property to **Dynaset**, **Dynaset (Inconsistent Updates)**, or **Snapshot**.

➤ **To modify the Control Source property**

1. Open the form in Design view, and then select the control you want to work with.

2. On the **Design** tool tab, in the **Tools** group, click **Property Sheet** (if the property sheet is not displayed).

3. On the property sheet's **Data** tab, click in the **Control Source** property box.

4. Select a different field from the list in the property box.

   Or

   Click the ellipsis to open the Expression Builder to create an expression for the control.

Sizing and ordering controls in Design view

In Design view, the Form Design Tools Arrange tool tab includes the Sizing & Ordering group. This group provides commands you can apply to controls to modify their size, the spacing between them, and their alignment. For example, if you want two or more text boxes to be the same size, select the text box controls, click Size/Space, and then click one of the options in the Size group. You can also use the Size/Space menu to control the spacing between controls and to group controls so that you can reposition the controls as a unit.

> **Tip** In the Grid section of the Size/Space menu, click Grid to show or hide the design grid. Temporarily hiding the grid displays the form's background more clearly. Click Ruler to hide or show the ruler. Keep Snap To Grid enabled to make positioning controls easier.

Use the Align command in the Sizing & Ordering group to align a group of controls at the left, right, top, or bottom. First select the controls, and then select the alignment option you want to apply. The Left option, for example, aligns the left borders of the controls with the control farthest to the left. The Bring To Front and Send To Back commands change the relationship of objects that overlap on a form.

➤ **To size and space controls in Design view**

1. In the Navigation pane, right-click the form, and then click **Design View**.

2. Select the control or controls you want to work with.

3. On the **Form Design Tools Arrange** tool tab, in the **Sizing & Ordering** group, click **Size/Space**, and then click the option you want to apply to the controls.

➤ **To align controls in Design view**

1. In the Navigation pane, right-click the form, and then click **Design View**.

2. Select the control or controls you want to work with.

3. On the **Arrange** tab, in the **Sizing & Ordering** group, click **Align**, and then click the option you want to apply to the controls.

➤ **To change the order of controls**

1. In the Navigation pane, right-click the form, and then click **Design View**.

2. Select the control or controls you want to work with.

3. On the **Arrange** tab, in the **Sizing & Ordering** group, click **Send to Back** or **Bring to Front**.

Working with control layouts in Layout view

In Layout view, a form's controls are contained within a layout that helps manage the alignment and arrangement of the controls. For desktop database forms, Access provides two default layouts. In the *tabular* layout, controls are arranged in columns and rows (something like a spreadsheet or a table). Labels are displayed in the form's Header section (like column headings). Access places the text box controls in the form's Detail section. In the *stacked* layout, controls appear in two columns, with labels in the column at the left and text box controls at the right. All controls in the stacked layout are included in a single form section. Access uses the stacked layout for forms you create by using the Form command and for blank forms you create in Layout view (by clicking Blank Form on the Create tab). You can switch between the tabular and stacked layouts by selecting a layout option in the Table group on the Form Layout Tools Arrange tool tab.

> **Tip** In Design view, you can remove a layout by selecting the controls on the form and then clicking Remove Layout in the Table group. In Layout view, you can right-click a control, point to Layout, and then click Remove Layout. (In Layout view, Remove Layout does not appear in the Table group.)

You can also use the Gridlines command in the Table group to display gridlines on a form. The options are Both, Horizontal, Vertical, Top, Bottom, or None. None is the default selection in Layout view. Adding gridlines by selecting one of the other options helps highlight certain controls and other information. Use the Color, Width, and Border options at the bottom of the Gridlines menu to change how gridlines appear.

The commands in the Rows & Columns group let you expand the area of a layout by inserting rows or columns. To add a row to a layout, select a cell that's adjacent to where you want the new row's location, and click Insert Above or Insert Below. Similarly, select an adjacent cell, and then click Insert Left or Insert Right to insert a column. To delete a row or column, right-click a cell in the row or column you want to delete, and then click Delete Row or Delete Column.

Another way to alter the arrangement of a layout is to merge or split cells. By merging cells, one control spans two columns or rows. After selecting the cells you want to merge, click Merge in the Merge/Split group. In contrast, when you split a cell in a layout, you can place two controls in that cell. Use the Split Horizontally or Split Vertically command to split cells.

By using the Move Up and Move Down commands in the Move group, you can reposition rows or a single cell in a layout. Click a cell in the row you want to move, click Select Row in the Rows & Columns group, and then click Move Up or Move Down.

The three commands in the Arrange tool tab's Position group adjust the spacing between controls, the margins around the text displayed by a control, and how controls are anchored within the layout. Each setting on the Control Margins menu—None, Narrow, Medium, and Wide—progressively increases the space between the upper-left corner of a control and the position of the control's text. The Wide setting can obscure text in a text box that is shorter than approximately .3 inches in height (assuming the font size you are using is the default 11 points).

Settings in the Control Padding area (also None, Narrow, Medium, and Wide) affect the space between controls in the layout. Click Select Layout in the Rows & Columns group, click Control Padding, and then click the padding option you want to apply.

Resizing a form's window can affect how controls are arranged. By using one of the anchoring options that Access provides, you can fasten controls to the top left (the default position), top right, bottom left, or one of the other anchoring positions. After you select an option on the Anchoring menu, resize the form window to test the effect. You can anchor the entire layout or specific elements on a form. For example, if you add a line to set off a section of a form, apply the Stretch Across Top anchoring option to have the line stretch across the top of the form when the form window is resized.

➤ **To work with control layouts in Layout view**

1. In the Navigation pane, right-click the form, and then click **Layout View**.

2. Click the **Form Layout Tools Arrange** tool tab.

3. To apply a different default layout to the form, click **Stacked** or **Tabular** in the **Table** group.

4. To insert a row or column in the layout, click a cell in the adjacent row or column, click **Select Row** or **Select Column** in the **Rows & Columns** group, and then click **Insert Above** or **Insert Below** (for rows), or **Insert Left** or **Insert Right** (for columns).

5. To merge two cells in the layout, select the cells, and then click **Merge** in the **Merge/Split** group.

6. To reposition a row in the layout, click a cell in the row, click **Select Row** in the **Rows & Columns** group, and then click **Move Up** or **Move Down** in the **Move** group.

7. To specify margins for a control or the layout, select the control or click **Select Layout** in the **Rows & Columns** group. In the **Position** group, click **Control Margins**, and then click the option you want to apply.

8. To insert padding for a control or the layout, select the control or click **Select Layout** in the **Rows & Columns** group. In the **Position** group, click **Control Padding**, and then click the option you want to apply.

9. To apply an anchoring option to the layout, click **Select Layout** in the **Rows & Columns** group. In the **Position** group, click **Anchoring**, and then choose the option you want to apply.

Managing labels

By default, Access includes a label when you add a control that can display data on a form. You can also use a label control for headings and to display descriptive or instructive text blocks on a form.

A label's Caption property is set by Access to match the Caption property set for a related field. Change the text displayed in a label by selecting the label and then clicking in the label control. You can then edit the label's text. (Access resizes the label to display the modified caption.)

For a specific form, you can define the properties for a label control and then use those properties as default settings. (You can also set default control properties for other types of controls.)

Add a label to a form, and then use the Format tool tab and the property sheet to define the label as you want it to appear. Some properties you might set include Fore Color, Background Color, Border Style, and Border Color. Click Set Control Defaults in the Controls group on the Design tool tab while this label is selected. New labels you place on the form will use the new default settings.

➤ **To update default settings for a label**

1. Open a form in Design view or Layout view.

2. Add a label control to the form, and then use options on the **Form Design Tools Format** tool tab (or the **Form Layout Tools Format** tool tab) and the property sheet to format the label as you want it to appear.

3. On the **Form Design Tools Design** tool tab (or **Form Layout Tools Design** tool tab), in the **Controls** group, click **More**, and then click **Set Control Defaults**.

Practice tasks

The practice files for these tasks are located in the MOSAccess2013\Objective4 practice file folder. You can save the results of the tasks in the same folder.

- Open the *Marketing_4* database.

- Open the *Campaign Information* form in Design view. Use the commands in the Sizing & Ordering group to align the labels to the left and to resize the text boxes so that they match the size of narrowest one. Use the Spacing options on the Size/Space menu to apply equal vertical space between the controls. Save the form when you finish these tasks.

- Open the *Marketing Materials* form in Layout view. Insert a new column to the right, and then use the field list to add the *Headline*, *Presentation*, and *Sales Kit* fields to the form. Adjust the margins and the control padding so that both are set to Medium. Do the following:

  - Add a command button control to the *Marketing Materials* form. Using the control wizard, set up the button so that it opens the *Task Details* form.

  - Add a hyperlink control to the *Marketing Materials* form. Set up the hyperlink so that it sends a message to your email address.

  - Using the *Marketing Materials* form, change settings for the Record Source Type property to understand how these changes affect how you can use the form to insert and update data.

- Open the *Tasks Details* form in Layout view or Design view. Do the following:

  - Change the font for the text box controls to Calibri. Apply bold formatting to the *Description* field. Do the following:

  - Apply the Short Date format to the *Start Date* and *Due Date* fields.

  - Select the New Task command button, and then use the Quick Styles and Change Shape commands to format the button.

4.3 Format forms

This section explains some of the formatting features you can apply to a form. For example, it covers how to modify the tab order—the order in which you can move between controls by pressing Tab. It describes how to apply a theme to a form, how to insert images, and how to modify a form's background. This section also covers form properties related to sorting records in a form and printing a form.

Setting the tab order for forms

The tab order determines the sequence in which controls gain focus as a user moves from field to field by pressing Tab. Carefully setting the tab order for a form can help users enter data in a logical manner (for example, first name, last name, and then middle initial instead of first name, street address, city, and then last name).

Access sets a default tab order as you add controls to a form, but this order may not be the most efficient. You can specify the tab order you want to use by working in the Tab Order dialog box or by setting the Tab Index and Tab Stop properties in the property sheet.

The Tab Order dialog box lists each section of the form and the fields and controls within that section. The fields are listed in the current tab order. As the dialog box explains, select a row (or multiple rows) and then drag the row or rows to the tab position you want to use.

```
                              Tab Order              ?   ×

 Click to select a row, or click   Custom Order:
 and drag to select multiple
 rows.  Drag selected row(s) to    │ Company                        │
 move them to desired tab          │ First Name                     │
 order.                            │ Last Name                      │
                                   │ Job Title                      │
                                   │ Business Phone                 │
                                   │ Mobile Phone                   │
                                   │ Fax Number                     │
                                   │ Address                        │
                                   │ City                           │
                                   │ State/Province                 │
                                   │ ZIP/Postal Code                │
                                   │ Country/Region                 │
                                   │ Attachments                    │
                                   │ E-mail Address                 │
                                   │ Web Page                       │
                                   │ Notes                          │
                                   │                                │

        OK              Cancel              Auto Order
```

To specify tab position in the property sheet, select a control, and then open the Other tab on the property sheet. Use the Tab Index property to specify the order of controls, starting with 0 (zero) for the first control. If you want to exclude a control from the tab order, set the Tab Stop property to No.

When you press Tab in the last control in the tab order, Access by default displays the next record in the form's record source and then moves the focus to the first field in the tab order. You can use the Cycle property for a form to change this behavior. The Cycle property appears on the Other tab in the property sheet for the form. The All Records setting provides the default behavior. Select Current Record to return the focus to the first field in the tab order for the current record. Select Current Page to move the focus to the first field in the tab order on the current page. (The Current Page setting applies to multipage forms.)

To create a tab order that moves between controls as they are placed left to right and top to bottom on a form, open the Tab Order dialog box, and then click Auto Order.

➤ **To set the tab order for a form**

1. In the Navigation pane, right-click the form, and then click **Design View**.

2. On the **Form Design Tools Design** tool tab, in the **Tools** group, click **Tab Order**.

3. In the **Tab Order** dialog box, select the field or fields whose tab order you want to set, and then drag the field or fields to the tab position you want to use.

4. Click **Auto Order** to arrange the tab order to match the order of the form's controls arranged left to right and top to bottom.

5. Click **OK**.

Formatting print layouts

If you create a form that you expect to print, you should consider the setting for the Layout For Print property. Setting this property to Yes or No determines whether Access uses screen fonts or printer fonts. *Screen fonts* are installed on your computer for on-screen display. They usually display type at a lower resolution than printer fonts. *Printer fonts* use design methods by which they more accurately represent the characters in a font. (When you set up a printer, the printer might install additional screen fonts. The fonts available are those installed as part of your printer's setup and depend on your printer.)

The appearance of characters and symbols displayed with a screen font can differ some-what when they are printed. For example, you might design a form on a system that uses a printer different from the one you use to print a form. When you print the form, Access displays a message indicating that the form was designed for another type of printer. If you proceed to print the form, your printer might substitute different fonts.

The Layout For Print property appears near the bottom of the list of properties on the property sheet's Format tab. (Be sure to select Form from the Selection Type list to display the correct list of properties.) The default setting for the property is No, which specifies that printer fonts installed on your computer will not be available for any font settings. Screen fonts and TrueType fonts are available. Specifying Yes makes screen fonts unavailable; printer fonts and TrueType fonts are available. (*TrueType* fonts are a printer font format that appear accurately on the screen and on many ink jet printers. TrueType fonts do not display as well on other printing platforms, such as certain PostScript printers.

See Also For more information about printing from Access databases, see section 1.5, "Print and export databases."

➤ **To set the Layout For Print property**

1. Open the form in Design view or Layout view.

2. On the **Form Design Tools Design** tool tab (or **Form Layout Tools Design** tool tab), in the **Tools** group, click **Property Sheet**.

3. On the property sheet's **Format** tab, click in the **Layout for Print** box, and then select the setting you want.

Sorting records

When you base a form on a table or a query, the form inherits any sort order defined for its record source. You can change the sort order for the records in a form without changing the sort order specified in its record source. To do this, you use the Order By and Order By On Load properties.

These properties appear on the Data tab in a form's property sheet. In the Order By property, enter the name of the field (enclosed in brackets) by which you want to sort the records. You can use more than one field by separating field names with a comma. By default, records are sorted in ascending order. Enter *DESC* after a field's names to sort in descending order.

The setting you specify for the Order By property is saved with the form, but the sort order is not automatically applied when you open the form unless you set Order By On Load to Yes.

> **Tip** When you have a form open in Datasheet view, you can sort records by selecting a field and then clicking the appropriate Sort button in the Sort & Filter group on the Home tab.

➤ **To set the Order By and Order By On Load properties**

1. Open the form in Design view or Layout view.

2. On the **Form Design Tools Design** tool tab (or **Form Layout Tools Design** tool tab), in the **Tools** group, click **Property Sheet**.

3. On the property sheet's **Data** tab, click in the **Order By** box, and then enter the name of the field or fields you want to sort by, enclosing the field names in brackets and separating field names by using a comma.

4. To sort a field in descending order, enter *DESC* after the field's name.

5. To sort the records when the form is opened, set **Order By On Load** to **Yes**.

Applying themes to a form

Themes are used throughout Office 2013 to provide a common look to documents, spreadsheets, presentations, and database objects. In Access, *themes* control colors and fonts. For forms, themes affect the color and font used in the form header and the font used in labels and text box controls.

You apply a theme to a form by using the Themes gallery, which Access displays when you click Themes on the Design tool tab in Design view or Layout view. When the Live Preview feature is enabled, a preview of a theme is displayed when you point to an option in the gallery.

> **Tip** If Live Preview is not enabled, click Options on the File tab. On the General page of the Access Options dialog box, select Enable Live Preview.

By default, the Themes gallery is divided into two groups. The In This Database group shows the default database theme and any other theme applied to a database object. The Office group lists the themes that Access provides. Click Browse For Themes at the bottom of the Themes gallery to locate other theme files (which use the .thmx file name extension). These themes might be available on your network or in a different folder on your local computer.

When you apply a theme to a form, that theme is inherited by other objects in the database. Applying a theme to all the objects in your database in a single step saves time, but you can also apply a theme to a single object or change the theme for a set of objects that share a theme. Click Themes to expand the Themes gallery, right-click a theme, and then choose one of the following options:

- Apply Theme To All Matching Objects
- Apply Theme To This Object Only
- Make This Theme The Database Default

When you apply a theme to a specific object, Access lists this theme in the In This Database group in the Themes gallery. A ScreenTip identifies which object the theme applies to or whether the theme applies to the database.

You aren't bound by the formatting in a theme. To apply a different color scheme to a form, click Colors in the Themes group, and then select the option you want to use. To update objects that use the same theme, right-click an option in the built-in colors list, and then choose Apply Color Scheme To All Matching Objects. You can also modify the font used in a form by clicking the Fonts command in the Themes group and then applying an option.

If you specify a different color scheme or font for a form, you can save those settings as a new theme. Open the form that includes the formatting you want to save. Click Themes on the Design tool tab, and then click Save Current Theme. The themes you define and save are displayed in the Themes gallery in their own group, named Custom.

➤ **To apply a theme to a form**

1. In the Navigation pane, right-click the form, and then click **Design View** or **Layout View**.

2. On the **Form Design Tools Design** tool tab (or the **Form Layout Tools Design** tool tab), click **Themes**, and then select the theme you want to apply to the form.

➤ **To modify the color scheme for a theme**

1. In the Navigation pane, right-click the form, and then click **Design View** or **Layout View**.

2. On the **Design** tool tab, click **Colors** in the **Themes** group, and then select the color scheme you want to use.

➤ **To define and apply your own color scheme**

1. On the **Design** tool tab, click **Colors** in the **Themes** group, and then click **Customize Colors**.

2. In the **Create New Theme Colors** dialog box, specify the colors for the theme elements (such as **Text/Background—Dark 1**).

3. Enter a name for the custom color scheme, and then click **Save**.

4. In the **Themes** group, click **Colors**, and then select the custom color scheme you want to apply.

➤ **To modify the font scheme for a theme**

1. In the Navigation pane, right-click the form, and then click **Design View** or **Layout View**.

2. On the **Design** tool tab, click **Fonts** in the **Themes** group, and then select the font scheme you want to use.

➤ **To define and apply your own font scheme**

1. On the **Design** tool tab, click **Fonts** in the **Themes** group, and then click **Customize Fonts**.

2. In the **Create New Theme Fonts** dialog box, specify the heading font and body font.

3. Enter a name for the custom font scheme, and then click **Save**.

4. In the **Themes** group, click **Fonts**, and then select the custom font scheme you want to apply.

Modifying a form's background

In Layout view and Design view, the Background group on the Design Tools Format tool tab includes two commands: Background Image and Alternate Row Color.

To use an image as the background for a form, click Background Image, click Browse, and then open the location where the image file is stored. After you add the image, you can set properties for the image to modify how Access displays it. Open the property sheet, click the property sheet's Format tab, and then set the following properties to control the display of a background image (the settings in one or more of these properties affect the options for others):

- **Picture Type** Use the Embedded option if you want Access to add a copy of the image to the form. With this option, you know the image is available whenever you load the form, but adding a copy of the image increases the size of the form and the database. If you choose Link, Access uses the path and file name specified in the Picture property to locate the image file each time you open the form. If the file is moved, Access can't display it until you update the path. If you use the Shared option, Access adds a copy of the image to a system table. You can then select the image from the Picture property list to display it as a background in other database objects.

- **Picture** This property specifies the image file used as the background. Choose an image from the list, or click the ellipsis if you want to select a different image file.

- **Picture Tiling** If you set the Picture Size Mode property to Clip or Zoom, and the image you insert is smaller than the form's dimensions, set this property to Yes to display multiple copies of the image on the form.

- **Picture Alignment** When the Picture Size Mode property is set to Clip or Zoom, choose an option in the Picture Alignment property to center the image or place it in a corner of the form.

- **Picture Size Mode** This property controls the size at which Access displays the image. The options include the following:

    ○ **Clip** Access trims the borders of the image so that it fits the size of the form.

○ **Zoom** Access increases or decreases the size of the image to fit the size of the form. With this option, Access retains the proportions of the image.

○ **Stretch, Stretch Horizontal, Stretch Vertical** When you choose one of these options, Access resizes the image to fit the size of the form, but the image's proportions can be distorted.

You can use the Alternate Row Color button with a form open in Datasheet view to apply a color you specify (a theme color, a standard color, or a color you define) to alternating rows in the datasheet. Access displays a form in Datasheet view when you select Datasheet in the Default View property for the form or you select Datasheet as the layout option when you use the Form wizard. When you open the form, the Alternate Row Color command is available on the Form Tools Datasheet tool tab.

➤ **To add an image to a form's background**

1. Open the form in Layout view or Design view.

2. Click the **Form Design Tools Format** tool tab (or the **Form Layout Tools Design** tool tab).

3. In the **Background** group, click **Background Image**.

4. Select an image in the **Image** gallery, or click **Browse** to locate the image file you want to use.

5. Select the image file in the **Insert Picture** dialog box, and then click **OK**.

➤ **To set properties for a background image**

1. Open the form in Layout view or Design view.

2. On either **Design** tool tab, click **Property Sheet**.

3. In the property sheet, select **Form** from the **Selection Type** list.

4. Set the values you want to use for the following properties: **Picture Type**, **Picture**, **Picture Tiling**, **Picture Alignment**, and **Picture Size Mode**.

➤ **To use an alternating row color**

1. Open the form in Datasheet view.

2. On the **Form Tools Datasheet** tool tab, click **Alternate Row Color**, and then choose the color you want to apply.

Using a form header and footer

As described in section 4.1, "Create forms," a form includes three sections: Detail, Header, and Footer. You can use the Header/Footer group on the Form Design Tools Design tool tab (or Forms Layout Tools Design tool tab) to insert a logo, a title, and the date and time in your form.

The commands in the Header/Footer group insert built-in elements, but you can add other controls to a form's header or footer by dragging the appropriate control to that section of the form. For example, you can add button controls to the header or footer section to save room for text boxes and other controls in the Detail section.

➤ **To insert information in a form header or footer**

1. In the Navigation pane, right-click the form and then choose **Design View** or **Layout View**.

2. On the **Form Design Tools Design** tool tab (or **Form Layout Tools Design** tool tab), in the **Header/Footer** group, click the option for the element you want to add to the form.

   ○ **Logo** Select the image file from the **Insert Picture** dialog box.

   ○ **Title** Enter a title for the form in the label control that Access provides.

   ○ **Date and Time** Specify the date and time format you want to use in the **Date and Time** dialog box.

Inserting images

Forms can display logos or images related to the purpose of the database—product thumbnails, project locations, or employee portraits, for example. To add an image to a form, open the form in Layout view or Design view, click Insert Image in the Design tool tab's Controls group, and then use the Insert Picture dialog box to specify the image file.

As you do with form backgrounds, you should update settings for the following properties that affect the appearance and behavior of the image: Picture Type, Picture, Picture Tiling, Picture Alignment, and Picture Size Mode.

> **See Also** For more information about how to use these properties, see the "Modifying a form's background" topic earlier in this section.

➤ **To insert an image on a form**

1. In the Navigation pane, right-click the form, and then click **Design View** or **Layout View**.

2. On the **Form Design Tools Design** tool tab (or the **Form Layout Tools Design** tool tab), in the **Controls** group, click **Insert Image**, and then click **Browse** to open the **Insert Picture** dialog box.

3. In the **Insert Picture** dialog box, select the image file, and then click **OK**.

4. On the **Design** tool tab, click **Property Sheet**.

5. In the property sheet, select **Form** in the **Selection Type** list.

6. Set the values you want to use for the following properties: **Picture Type**, **Picture**, **Picture Tiling**, **Picture Alignment**, and **Picture Size Mode**.

Practice tasks

The practice files for these tasks are located in the MOSAccess2013\Objective4 practice file folder. You can save the results of the tasks in the same folder.

- Open the *Marketing_4* database.

- Open the *Tasks Details* form in Design view, and apply the Organic theme to the form. Use the Colors and Fonts commands to modify the elements of the theme, and then save the modified theme as a custom theme.

- Add a background image to the *Task Details* form by using one of the image files available on your computer.

- Open the *CampaignInformation* form in Design view. Open the Tab Order dialog box, and modify the form's tab order.

- Using the *CampaignInformation* form, sort the form's records in descending order by country.

Objective review

Before finishing this chapter, be sure you have mastered the following skills:

4.1 Create a form

4.2 Set form controls

4.3 Format forms

5 Create reports

The skills tested in this section of the Microsoft Office Specialist exam for Microsoft Access 2013 relate to creating reports. Specifically, the following objectives are associated with this set of skills:

5.1 Create a report

5.2 Set report controls

5.3 Format reports

You can use reports to create a view of your data, to group and summarize data, and to provide data in a format that's suitable for sharing, printing, and presentations. As with forms, you build reports by adding fields from one or more tables or queries. You can format reports to emphasize data and enhance their appearance by adding graphics, logos, titles, and descriptive labels.

> **Important** Forms and reports have many characteristics in common, and many of the tools you use to modify the design and formatting of reports are the same as you use to modify forms. You should be sure to study Chapter 4, "Create forms," for detailed information about topics such as working in Layout view, using the field list, and creating custom themes. Throughout this chapter are references that point you to sections in Chapter 4 that provide more detailed descriptions of these and other topics.

An important step in setting up many reports is defining how you want Access to group records. For example, in a report summarizing a product list by supplier, Access inserts a group header for each supplier's name and can then list and sort that supplier's products within each group.

Like forms, reports contain several sections, including Page Header, Detail, and Page Footer. In the Page Header section, you can include labels that identify the data fields in the Detail section, for example. Use the Page Footer section to display page numbers and similar information. A report can also include the Report Header and Report Footer sections. The Report Header section appears only on the first page of a report and can be used to display a title or a logo. The Report Footer section appears at the end of the report. Use this section to display a grand total of values on the report.

You can view completed reports in Print Preview or Report view. Print Preview is a static view that shows how the report's printed pages will appear—for example, whether the margins are set correctly, whether formatting is in place, and whether the information you want in the report's header and footer sections is included. The Print Preview tab that Access displays in this view includes a Print button, the Page Size and Page Layout groups, the Zoom group, and the Data group. You can use options in the Data group to export a report to Microsoft Excel, to a text file, as a PDF or XPS document, in email, and in other formats.

> **See Also** For more information about working with Print Preview in Access, see section 1.5, "Print and export databases."

Report view is a more interactive view. In Report view, hyperlinks are enabled, and you can also apply a filter to a report. After you apply a filter, you can print the filtered report to show only that subset of data.

This chapter guides you in studying how to use the tools for creating reports. This chapter also describes how to organize and format report controls, how to group and sort data in reports, and how to format reports, including how to specify page setup and layout options.

> **Practice Files** To complete the practice tasks in this chapter, you need the practice file contained in the MOSAccess2013\Objective5 practice file folder. For more information, see "Download the practice files" in this book's Introduction.

5.1 Create a report

The options for creating reports on the ribbon's Create tab are Report, Report Design, Blank Report, Report Wizard, and Labels.

The Report command uses all the fields in the table or query you select in the Navigation pane to build a basic report that Access opens in Layout view. On the Report Layout Tools Design tool tab, in the Views group, click Report View or Print Preview to display the report as is. Use the commands on the Design tool tab and on the Report Layout Tools Arrange and Format tool tabs to insert additional fields and controls, group and sort records, change the report's layout, add a background image, and make other changes to the report's design and formatting. Use the Report Layout Tools Page Setup tool tab to change the page size, page orientation, or margins. Later sections in this chapter cover tools and options on the Design, Arrange, Format, and Page Setup tool tabs in more detail.

The Report wizard leads you through options for how to group, sort, and summarize the records in a report and provides a choice of layouts. If you want to create a report from scratch, click Blank Report to work in Layout view, or click Report Design to create the report in Design view.

> **Tip** To modify reports already included in a database, right-click the report in the Navigation pane, and then click Design View or Layout View, depending on which view you want to work with. Use the procedures described in the "Building reports in Layout view" topic and the "Using report design tools" topic later in this section to make changes to the report's fields, properties, and formatting.

The Labels command displays a wizard that creates labels for an address list (similar to the mail merge operation in Microsoft Word.) You provide information such as label size, font attributes, and the data fields to include on the labels.

> **See Also** For information about adding reports to your database by using application parts, see the "Working with application parts" topic in section 1.1, "Create new databases."

Running the Report wizard

Run the Report wizard when you want help creating a report that includes fields from more than one table or query. After you select the fields for the report, the wizard prompts you to specify how you want to view the records in the report. The option you choose determines the first grouping level for the report. For example, you can choose By Suppliers or By Products for a report that includes fields from both of these tables. The wizard displays a preview that shows how the report's records will be organized. Base your decision on the view of the data you want the report to provide. In this example, the report can display which products each supplier provides or all suppliers for individual products.

You can select additional fields to use as grouping levels. Click Grouping Options to open a dialog box in which you set the grouping interval. Grouping intervals depend on a field's data type. For a Date/Time field, you can use an interval such as year or quarter. For a numeric field, you can specify an incremental value such as 1,000. You can use text fields to group by a specific number of letters.

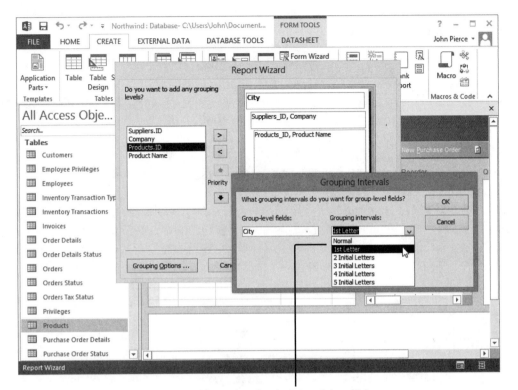

The options for the intervals by which you
group records depend on a field's data type.
The options shown here are for a text field.

In the wizard, you can specify as many as four fields by which to sort data. You can use
only those fields not specified for a grouping level. On the page where you specify the
report's sort order, click Summary Options to select a function, such as Sum or Average,
that Access uses to summarize report data. On this page, you can choose between showing only summary data or both detail records (for example, itemized expenses in a specific budget category) and summary data (the total for that category).

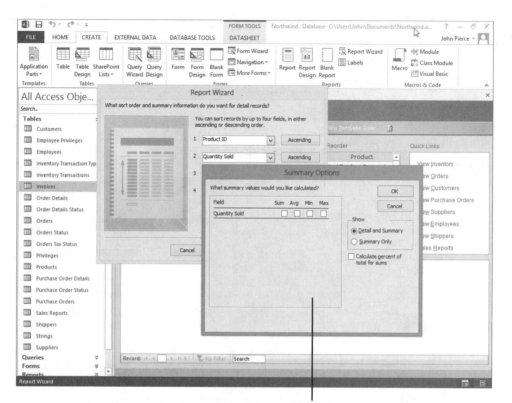

After specifying the sort order for a report, use the Summary
Options dialog box to select a summary function and to choose
an option to show only summary values or both details and a summary

For the layout for the report, choose Stepped, Block, or Outline. A preview shows how each option affects the layout of the report. You can also select portrait or landscape orientation and specify whether the wizard should adjust the width of each field so that fields fit on the page. Selecting the option to adjust field width might cause some text boxes to display only a portion of the field's data.

➤ **To create a report with the Report wizard**

1. On the **Create** tab, in the **Reports** group, click **Report Wizard**.

2. Use the **Tables/Queries** list to select the report's record source, add the fields you want to use to the **Selected Fields** list, and then click **Next**.

3. Specify the field or fields by which you want to group records in the report. Click **Grouping Options** to specify the interval by which to group dates, numeric values, or text fields, and then click **Next**.

4. Choose the field or fields you want to use to sort records. Click **Summary Options** to specify the summary function you want to apply and to choose an option to view only summary data or both detail and summary data, and then click **Next**.

5. Choose a report layout and a page orientation, and then click **Next**.

6. Enter a name for the report, choose whether to preview the report or open the report in Design view, and then click **Finish**.

Building reports in Layout view

The Blank Report command opens an empty page in Layout view and displays the field list. (Click Show All Tables in the field list if no tables are shown.) To add fields to the report, in the field list, expand the list of fields for a table, and then drag a field to the report page or double-click the field.

In Layout view, a report's controls are contained within a layout that helps manage the alignment and arrangement of controls. For reports, Access provides two default layouts: tabular and stacked.

In the *tabular* layout, controls are arranged in columns and rows (something like a spreadsheet). Labels are displayed in the report's Page Header section (similar to column headings). Text box controls that display a field's data are included in the report's Detail section. In the *stacked* layout, controls appear in two columns, with labels in the left column and field controls in the right column. All controls in the stacked layout are included in a report's Detail section.

By default, Access uses the tabular layout for reports it creates with the Report tool and for blank forms you create in Layout view. When you add the first field, Access displays a button (identified by a lightning bolt icon) beside the field. You can click this button to switch the report from the tabular layout to the stacked layout. You can also switch between the tabular and stacked layouts by selecting the layout from the Table group on the Report Layout Tools Arrange tool tab.

> **Tip** When a report is open in Design view, you can remove a layout by selecting the controls on the report and then clicking the Remove Layout command in the Table group on the Arrange tool tab. If you are creating a report in Layout view, you can right-click a control, point to Layout, and then click Remove Layout. (In Layout view, the Remove Layout command does not appear in the Table group.)

In Layout view, click this button to switch
from tabular layout to stacked layout

Layout view displays data from the underlying record source, but you cannot update the data in the report window. Click Edit Table in the field list to open the table in Datasheet view to work with the data itself.

When you work in Layout view, the Design, Arrange, Format, and Page Setup tool tabs appear under Report Layout Tools. As you add and arrange fields, use options on these tabs to refine the report's layout and appearance. For example, you can apply a theme to change the font and color scheme for the report, or use commands on the Format tab to add details such as colored fills or outlines to a control. On the Design tool tab, use the Grouping & Totals group to group and sort records, add totals, and hide details. Use the Header/Footer group on the Design tool tab to add a title, logo, or date and time to the report.

Use the commands in the Rows & Columns group on the Arrange tool tab when you need to expand the area of a layout by inserting rows or columns. To add a row to a layout, first select an adjacent cell, and then click Insert Above or Insert Below. Similarly, select an adjacent cell, and then click Insert Left or Insert Right in the Rows & Columns group to insert a column. To delete a row or column, right-click a cell in that row or column and then click Delete Row or Delete Column.

Another way to alter the arrangement of a layout is to merge or split cells. By merging cells, you can have one control span two columns or rows. After selecting the cells you want to merge, click Merge in the Merge/Split group. In contrast, when you split a cell in a layout, you can place two controls in that cell. Use the Split Horizontally or Split Vertically command to split cells.

By using the Move Up and Move Down commands in the Arrange tab's Move group, you can reposition the rows or a single cell in a layout. Click a cell in the row you want to move, click Select Row in the Rows & Columns group, and then click Move Up or Move Down.

The two commands in the Arrange tool tab's Position group adjust spacing between controls and the margins around the text a control displays. Each setting on the Control Margins menu (None, Narrow, Medium, and Wide) progressively increases the space between the upper-left corner of a control and the position where the control's text appears. The Wide setting can obscure text in a text box that is anything less than approximately .3 inches in height (assuming the font size specified is the default 11 points).

Settings on the Control Padding menu (also None, Narrow, Medium, and Wide) adjust the space between controls in the layout. Click Select Layout in the Rows & Columns group, click Control Padding, and then choose the padding option you want to apply.

To specify report properties, click Property Sheet on the Design tool tab. In the property sheet, you can set properties for each report section, for controls, and for the report itself. For example, set the Default View property for the report to Report View or Print Preview depending on how you want Access to display the report when you open it.

➤ **To create a report using Layout view**

1. On the **Create** tab, in the **Reports** group, click **Blank Report**.

2. In the field list, click **Show All Tables** (if no tables are shown), and then click the plus sign (+) beside the table you want to use as the report's record source. If the field list is not displayed, click **Add Existing Fields** on the **Report Layout Tools Design** tool tab.

3. From the field list, drag the fields you want to include on the report and place them in the report window. You can align and reposition fields after you place them.

4. To add a logo, title, or date and time to the report, use the commands in the **Header/Footer** group.

5. On the **Design** tool tab, click **Property Sheet**.

6. In the property sheet, specify properties for the report and the report's controls.

➤ **To work with control layouts in Layout view**

1. In the Navigation pane, right-click the report, and then click **Layout View**.

2. Click the **Report Layout Tools Arrange** tool tab.

3. To apply a different layout to the report, select all the fields in the report, and then, in the **Table** group, click **Stacked** or **Tabular**.

4. To adjust the report's layout, you can do the following:

   ○ To insert a row or column in the layout, click a cell in the adjacent row or column, click **Select Row** or **Select Column** in the **Rows & Columns** group, and then click **Insert Above** or **Insert Below** (for rows), or **Insert Left** or **Insert Right** (for columns).

   ○ To merge two cells in the layout, select the cells, and then click **Merge** in the **Merge/Split** group.

   ○ To reposition a row in the layout, click a cell in the row, click **Select Row** in the **Rows & Columns** group, and then click **Move Up** or **Move Down** in the **Move** group.

   ○ To specify margins for a control or the layout, select the control or click **Select Layout** in the **Rows & Columns** group. In the **Position** group, click **Control Margins**, and then select the option you want to apply.

   ○ To insert padding for a control or the layout, select the control or click **Select Layout** in the **Rows & Columns** group. In the **Position** group, click **Control Padding**, and then select the option you want to apply.

Using report design tools

The Report Design command opens a blank report page in Design view. The page shows three of the sections you can use in a report—Page Header, Detail, and Page Footer. Use the Add Existing Fields command in the Tools group on the Report Design Tools Design tool tab to display the field list. You can then expand the list of fields for the table you want to use as the report's record source and add fields to the report.

Use the grid marks and the ruler to align and position fields. Access highlights the ruler when you drag a control to indicate its relative position. By right-clicking a control, you can work with options for the Align, Size, and Position commands to adjust the placement and dimensions of controls. For example, to make a group of labels the same size, select the labels, right-click, point to Size, and then click To Tallest, To Widest, or one of the other sizing commands.

You often locate most of the report's controls in its Detail section, including labels and text boxes related to the report's data. The Page Header section displays information at the top of each page of a report. Use this section to show a date for a report or a heading such as *Internal Use Only* that you want to appear on each page. Information in the Page Footer section—page numbers, for example—appears at the bottom of each page. Information in the Report Header and Report Footer sections appears only once—at the top of the report's first page and at the bottom of the report's last page, respectively. You can use the Report Header section to display the report's title or to include a logo.

To display the Report Header and Report Footer sections, right-click in the Detail section and then click Report Header/Footer. You can also use the commands in the Header/Footer group on the Design tool tab to add information to these sections by inserting an element such as a title, a logo, a date, and page numbers. Right-clicking the Detail section and choosing Report/Header Footer a second time hides these sections of a report.

When you work in Design view (or in Layout view), you can add controls to a report to supplement the controls Access creates when you insert fields. For example, you might include additional labels, an image, or a subreport control that displays data from a related table or query.

> **See Also** For information about using subreports, see the "Using subreports" topic later in this section.

To add a control, click Controls on the Design tool tab, select the type of control you want to add, and then click on the page where you want to place the control.

> **See Also** For more information about working with controls and setting control properties, see section 4.2, "Set form controls," and the "Managing report fields and properties" topic of section 5.2, "Set report controls."

When you have a report open in Design view, the Report Design Tools Arrange tool tab includes the Sizing & Ordering group. This group provides commands you can apply to controls to modify their size, the spacing between them, and their alignment. For example, if you want two or more text boxes to have the same size, select the text box controls, click Size/Space, and then choose one of the options in the Size group. You can also use the Size/Space menu to control the spacing between controls and to group controls so that you can reposition the controls as a unit. Use the Align command in the Sizing & Ordering group to align a group of controls. The Bring To Front and Send To Back commands change the relationship of objects that overlap on a report.

➤ **To create a report in Design view**

1. On the **Create** tab, in the **Reports** group, click **Report Design**.

2. To display the field list, click **Add Existing Fields** in the **Tools** group on the **Report Design Tools Design** tool tab.

3. In the field list, click **Show All Tables** (if no tables are shown), and then click the plus sign (+) beside the table you want to use as the form's record source.

4. From the field list, drag the fields you want to include on the report and place them in the report window. You can align and reposition fields after you place them.

5. To add a logo, title, or date and time to the report, use the commands in the **Header/Footer** group.

➤ **To arrange controls in Design view**

1. In the report, select the control or controls you want to work with.

2. On the **Report Design Tools Arrange** tool tab, in the **Sizing & Ordering** group, you can do the following to adjust the report's design:

   ○ To adjust the size and spacing between selected controls, click **Size/Space**, and then click the option you want to apply to the controls.

   ○ To align selected controls, click **Align**, and then click the option you want to apply to the controls.

   ○ To change the position of a control or selected controls, click **Send to Back** or **Bring to Front**.

Using subreports

You can insert a subreport into a main report to provide related information. You can create the subreport by using the Report wizard or you can define the subreport by using the Subreport wizard. In either case, the subreport must contain a field you can use to link it to the main report.

To add a subreport, follow the steps in the Subreport wizard, which appears when you add a subreport control to the report page. In the wizard, first select the report you want to use as the subreport or choose the option to base the subreport on an existing table or query. If you choose to work with a table or query, select the table or query and then add the fields you want to use. You then need to either select the set of linking fields that Access detects or define your own. After you name the subreport, click Finish in the wizard to add it to the main report.

➤ **To insert a subreport control**

1. Open the main report in Design view or Layout view.

2. On the **Report Design Tools Design** tool tab (or the **Report Layout Tools Design** tool tab), select the **Subform/Subreport** control in the **Controls** group, and then click in the main report where you want to place the subreport.

3. Follow the steps in the **Subreport** wizard to select the report, table, or query on which to base the subreport, select fields for the subreport, and specify the field that links the subreport and the main report.

Deleting reports

When you no longer need a report in a database, right-click the report in the Navigation pane, and then click Delete. Before you delete a report, consider using the External Data tab to export a report to create a snapshot of data at a particular time and to build your data archives.

Practice tasks

The practice files for these tasks are located in the MOSAccess2013\Objective5 practice file folder. You can save the results of the tasks in the same folder.

- Open the *Marketing_5* database.

- Use the Report command to create a report based on the *Expense Report* query (*qryExpenseReport*). Save this report with the name *Expense Summary*.

- Use the Report wizard to create a report by using the *Marketing Campaigns* and the *Campaign Expenses* tables. Group the report by campaign and expense type.

- Create a report in Layout view that includes fields from the *Marketing Campaigns* and *Campaign Expenses* tables. Apply the stacked layout to the report. Switch the report to Design view, and insert the *Report Header* and *Report Footer* sections. Add a title and the date to the *Report Header* section.

- Open the *Campaign Summary* report in Design view, and add the *Campaign Expenses subreport* to the main report. Position the subreport to the left of the *Task Summary* subreport.

5.2 Set report controls

This section describes how to work with fields and controls on a report. It explains how to add controls, select fields to group and sort records, and how to manage a report's data source. This section also covers some of the report and control properties you can set in the property sheet.

Adding controls to a report

Reports are designed primarily to present and share data (unlike forms or tables, which you use to enter, update, and delete data). You often work only with label and text box controls to identify and present data in a report. For example, you might add a label to identify a summary field in a group header section or to provide a title in the Report Header section. You can add a text box to a report and then write an expression to create a calculated field. You can add an image control to enhance the appearance of a report.

> **See Also** For more information about how to work with specific controls, see section 4.2, "Set form controls."

Although the data in a report is more static than in a form or a table, you can use a command button to perform an action related to the report or add a hyperlink control to display a website or an email address. In Report view, command buttons and hyperlinks are operational. In Print Preview, Access doesn't display a command button, and a hyperlink appears as static text.

➤ **To add controls to a report**

1. Open the report in Layout view or Design view.

2. On the **Report Design Tools Design** tool tab (or the **Report Layout Tools Design** tool tab), in the **Controls** group, click the type of control you want to add, and then click in the report page where you want to add the control.

Managing report fields and properties

Each control on a report, each report section, and the report itself has a group of properties that you can work with on the property sheet. (Click Property Sheet on the Report Design Tools Design tool tab to display the property sheet.) For example, you can set properties on the property sheet's Format tab to fine-tune the formatting for a control. For a text box, you can set properties such as Width, Height, Back Color, Border Style, Border Color, Font Name, Font Size, and Text Align.

Select a control or report section from this list
to format and design a report by using the property sheet

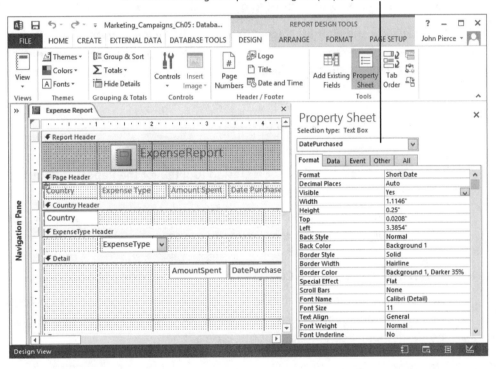

For report sections (such as Detail, Page Header, and Page Footer), you can set the Height property to 0" to hide the section. For the Detail section, set the Can Grow and Can Shrink properties to Yes if you want the size of the Detail section to increase and decrease depending on the amount of information it displays for a particular record. The Report Header and Report Footer sections also have these properties.

For the Report Header and Report Footer sections and the Page Header and Page Footer sections, you can also set the Display When property to Always, Print Only, or Screen Only. If you add page numbers to the Page Footer section, for example, set Display When to Print Only to show the page numbers only when you print the report.

Report properties include the Default View property, which controls whether the report opens in Print Preview or Report view by default. (The report opens in the view you specify for the Default View property when you right-click a report in the Navigation pane and then click Open.) The Grid Y and Grid X properties control the number and spacing of the dots in the design grid in Design view. If you use Design view frequently, set the values for Grid Y and Grid X to 10 or to 12 to more easily align controls on the grid.

You can view and alter the Record Source property for a report by displaying the property sheet's Data tab, clicking in the Record Source property box, and then pressing Shift+F2 to open the Zoom dialog box or clicking the ellipsis button (...) to view and change the record source in the Query Builder.

➤ **To set control and report properties**

1. Open the report in the Design view or Layout view.

2. On the **Report Design Tools Design** tool tab (or the **Report Layout Tools Design** tool tab), click **Property Sheet** in the **Tools** group.

3. Click in the box for the property you want to set, and then select an option Access provides or enter the value you want to use.

Formatting report controls

By working with the commands in the Font group on the Report Design Tools Format tool tab (or the Report Layout Tools Design tool tab), you can make changes to font properties for labels and other controls on a report.

> **Tip** When you are formatting controls on a report, use the list in the Selection group at the far left of the Format tab to select the control.

For example, click a label on a report and then select the font you want to use from the Font list. You can also change the size of the font, choose a different font color, or apply a background color to a control. Use the alignment buttons to position the text flush left, flush right, or centered.

In the Number group, you can apply a format to fields that use the Number, Currency, or Date/Time data type. For example, select a date field in the report, and then choose a format from the list provided. The format you choose here affects how the date is displayed, but it doesn't change the date format specified for the field in the table.

With the commands in the Control Formatting group, you can format controls in other ways. Use the Shape Fill command to add a background color to a control such as the report's title. The Shape Outline command lets you modify the color and style of a control's borders.

➤ **To format report controls**

1. Open the form in Layout view or Design view.

2. Click the **Report Design Tools Format** tool tab (or the **Report Layout Tools Format** tool tab).

3. In the **Selection** group, select the control you want to format or click **Select All**. (You can also click to select a control on the form.)

4. In the **Font** group, choose a new font, font size, or font color; apply bold, italic, or underline formatting; add a background fill color; and align the text.

5. For number, currency, and date and time fields, use the **Number** group to apply number, date/time, and currency formatting to the field.

6. In the **Control Formatting** group, do the following:

   ○ Use the **Shape Fill** command to add a background fill color to a control.

   ○ Use the **Shape Outline** command to apply line styles and colors to the control's borders.

Working with labels

When you add a text, number, or date field to a report, Access creates a text box to display the field's data and creates an associated label to display the field's name or caption. (Access also creates an associated label for other types of fields, including lookup fields and fields that use the AutoNumber data type). You can then use the techniques described earlier in this chapter to format, size, and position the labels to fit the report's design.

> **See Also** For more information, see the "Building reports in Layout view" and "Using report design tools" topics in section 5.1, "Create a report," and the "Adding controls to a report" and "Formatting report controls" topics earlier in this section.

To work with the full range of properties available for a label control, open the property sheet (from the Report Design Tools Design tool tab or the Report Layout Tools Design tool tab). Specify values on the property sheet's Format tab for properties such as Width, Height, Back Style, Special Effect, and Font Size. On the property sheet's Other tab, add a name for the label to replace the default name Access provides.

You can also add labels to a report (or a form) that aren't associated with fields. You might use a freestanding label to provide instructional text on a form or to provide a heading or other display text in a report.

When you add a label to the Detail section of a report by clicking Label in the Design tool tab's Controls gallery and then clicking the report, Access by default displays a trace error button. In the Detail section, labels in most cases are associated with controls that display data, so Access considers the addition of the label an error because it detects that the label is not associated with another control. Click this button, and then click Ignore Error if you don't want to create an association for this label. If you do want to create an association, click Associate Label With A Control to open the Associate Label dialog box. In the dialog box, select the control you want to associate with the label.

> **Tip** Access also displays the Trace Error button if you select a control and a label and Access detects that the label and the control aren't associated.

You can turn off the error-checking options related to labels in the Access Options dialog box. These options appear on the Object Designers page.

> **See Also** For information about setting a default format for labels, see section 4.2, "Set form controls."

➤ **To turn off error checking for labels**

1. Click the **File** tab, and then click **Options**.

2. In the **Access Options** dialog box, click the **Object Designers** category.

3. In the **Error checking in form and report design view** section, clear the **Check for unassociated label and control** and **Check for new unassociated labels** check boxes.

Modifying data sources

A report is tied to the data in a single table, multiple tables, or a query (which is itself based on one or more tables). Many report controls are bound to specific fields in the report's record source (also called its *data source*). When you create a report, Access builds the record source depending on tables and fields you select. You can also specify the record source yourself when you work in Design view or Layout view. The data source for a specific control is governed by its Control Source property. The Control Source property can be set to a specific field in the report's record source or to an expression. For example, you can add a text box to a report and then enter an expression such as =[City] & ", " & [State] & [Postal Code] to create the last line of an address block.

You can base a report (or multiple reports) on a query that you've designed and saved as an object in your database. However, if you modify the query, you might also affect the design of the report. To work around this possibility, you can embed a query in the report's Record Source property. An embedded query is not saved as a separate object, so any changes you make to the embedded query are also reflected in the report. Access creates an embedded query when you build a report in Layout view or Design view by adding fields from the field list. The Report wizard creates an embedded query when you select fields from more than one table.

To create or modify the record source for a report, open the property sheet and then click the property sheet's Data tab. You can choose a different table or query by clicking in the Record Source box and then selecting an object from the list of tables and queries in the database. Click the ellipsis button in the Record Source box to open the Query Builder (which is similar to the Query Designer described in detail in Chapter 3, "Create queries"). Use the Query Builder to add or remove fields for the current record source or to create the record source yourself.

When you open the Query Builder in a report that is based on a single table, Access prompts you to create a query based on the table, which converts the report's record source to an embedded query. In the Query Builder, drag the fields you want to include in the report from the table to the Field row in the design grid. (You can also double-click a field to add it to the design grid.) If you want to add fields from a related table, click Show Table on the Query Tools Design tool tab to open the Show Table dialog box. You can then select other tables or queries to add to the report's record source. After updating the record source, test the query by clicking Run on the Query Tools Design tool tab to open the query in Datasheet view.

> **Tip** You can save an embedded query as an object in your database by clicking Save As in the Close group on the Query Tools Design tool tab.

To modify the Control Source property for a specific control, open the property sheet and display its Data tab. Click in the Control Source box and then pick another field from the report's record source, or click the ellipsis to open the Expression Builder, which you can use to create an expression for a calculated control.

> **See Also** For more information about the Expression Builder, see section 3.3, "Utilize calculated fields and grouping within queries."

➤ **To modify a report's record source**

1. Open the report in Design view or Layout view.

2. On the **Report Design Tools Design** tool tab (or the **Report Layout Tools Design** tool tab), in the **Tools** group, click **Property Sheet** (if the property sheet is not displayed).

3. On the property sheet's **Data** tab, click in the **Record Source** box.

4. Select a different table or query from the list in the property box

   Or

   Click the ellipsis to open the Query Builder, use the Query Builder to modify the fields in the form's record source, and then close the Query Builder.

➤ **To modify the Control Source property**

1. Open the report in Design view or Layout view.

2. On the **Design** tool tab, in the **Tools** group, click **Property Sheet** (if the property sheet is not displayed).

3. On the property sheet's **Data** tab, click in the **Control Source** box.

4. Select a different field from the list in the property box, or click the ellipsis to open the Expression Builder to create an expression for the control.

Grouping and sorting fields

Specifying how records are grouped in a report is an important aspect of the report's design. You can set grouping levels when you use the Report wizard and by using the Group & Sort command when you create a report in Layout view or Design view. The

Grouping & Totals group on the Report Design Tools Design tool tab (or the Report Layout Tools Design tool tab) also includes the Totals command, which you use to summarize field values in a report.

When you click Group & Sort, Access displays the Group, Sort, And Total pane at the bottom of the report window. Click Add A Group, and then select the field you want to use for grouping. Access adds a group header section to the report that uses the name of the field you select. To add a grouping level, click Add A Group again and select another field.

If you work in Layout view, Access displays more clearly how the selections you make in the Group, Sort, And Total pane affect the report's organization. Access doesn't show this level of detail in Design view.

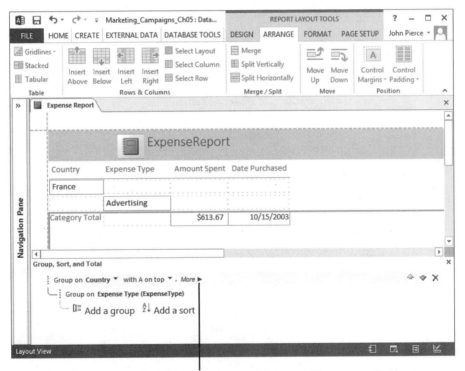

Click More to display additional options for how fields
on a report are grouped, sorted, and totaled

Click Add A Sort in the Group, Sort, And Total pane to sort records within each grouping level. For example, in a budget report, you could group records first by country or region and then sort records within that group by expense category. You could also group by expense category and sort records within that group by the date of the expense.

When you click More in the Group, Sort, And Total pane, Access displays additional options that you can set for grouping and sorting fields:

- **Sort Order** Use this option to specify the sort order, either ascending or descending.

- **Group Interval** Use this option to specify how records are grouped. You can group a text field on the first letter, for example, which would group all A items together, all B items, and so on. Date fields can be grouped by day, week, month, quarter, or an interval you define.

- **Totals** You can add totals for multiple fields and apply different summary functions (Sum and Avg or Min and Max, for example) to the same field. Use the Total On list to select a field, use the Type list to select the function, and then select the options you want to use to show the totals.

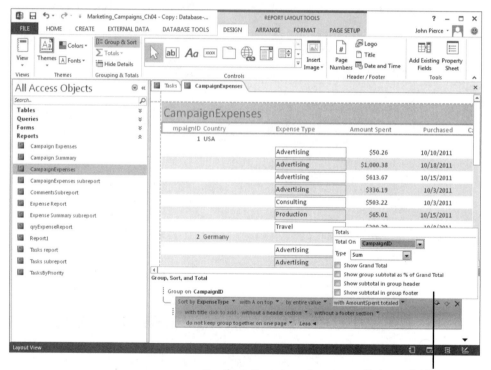

Use the options shown here to specify how a field's
summary values can be displayed in a report

- **Title** Use this option to change the title of the field being summarized. The title is used for the column heading and for labeling summary fields in headers and footers. Click the field link, and then enter the new title in the Zoom dialog box.

- **With/Without A Header Section** Use this setting to add or remove the header section for each group. Access moves the grouping field to the header when you add the header section. Access prompts you to remove any controls (other than the grouping field) from the header when you remove it.

- **With/Without A Footer Section** Use this setting to add or remove the footer section that follows each group. When you remove a footer section that contains controls, Access asks for confirmation to delete the controls.

- **Keep Group Together** The settings for this option determine how groups are laid out on the page when the report is printed.

To summarize the values in a field and add a text box that displays the summary value, click in the field you want to summarize and then click Totals in the Grouping & Totals group. The options available depend on the data type of the field you select. For numeric fields, the range of options include Sum, Average, Count, Max, and Min. For text and Date/Time fields, the Count options are available.

> **Tip** After you create a summary report, click Hide Details in the Grouping & Totals group to show only the summary fields.

➤ To group and sort records in a report

1. Open the report in Layout view or Design view.

2. On the **Report Design Tools Design** tool tab (or the **Report Layout Tools Design** tool tab), click **Group & Sort**.

3. In the **Group, Sort, and Total** pane, click **Add a group**, and then select the field to group by.

4. In the **Group, Sort, and Total** pane, click **More**, and then specify settings for sorting, grouping intervals, totals, title, header and footer sections, and how to keep groups together on the page.

➤ To summarize values on a report

1. Open the report in Layout view or Design view.

2. In the report, select the field you want to summarize.

3. On the **Design** tool tab, in the **Grouping & Totals** group, click **Totals**, and then choose the summary function you want to apply.

Practice tasks

The practice files for these tasks are located in the MOSAccess2013\Objective5 practice file folder. You can save the results of the tasks in the same folder.

- Open the *Marketing_5* database.

- Open the *Expense Summary* report you created in the practice tasks for section 5.1, "Create reports," in Layout view. (If you did not create this report, open the report named *Expense Summary_2* from the Navigation pane.)

- Group the report by expense type and country, and sort the report by date purchased. Use the Totals button to sum the *Amount Spent* field, and add the *Summary* field to the group footer.

- Open the property sheet. Select the Auto_Header control, and change its *Caption* property to *Expense Summary*.

- Create a report based on the *Marketing Campaigns* table. Use the Query Builder to convert the report's record source to an embedded query. Modify the record source by adding fields from the *Tasks* table and the *Campaign Expenses* table.

5.3 Format reports

You can use a variety of tools and techniques to format a report and the controls and other objects (such as images) that you include on a report. For example, you can add a background image, apply a theme to a report, or arrange a report's data in two or more columns. This section describes these and other aspects of formatting a report.

Applying themes to reports

In reports, themes provide font and color schemes. You can apply a built-in theme when you work with a report in Layout view or Design view. Choose a theme in the Themes gallery that Access displays when you click Themes on the Report Design Tools Design tool tab (or Report Layout Tools Design tool tab). If Live Preview is enabled, Access displays a preview of the theme as you hover your mouse pointer over the options in the gallery.

Tip If Live Preview is not enabled, click Options on the File tab. On the General page of the Access Options dialog box, select Enable Live Preview.

When you apply a theme to a report, that theme is inherited by other objects in the database. You can apply a different theme to a specific report or change the theme used by reports and other objects that share a common theme. To apply a theme to database objects, right-click a theme in the gallery, and then click one of the following options:

- Apply Theme To All Matching Objects
- Apply Theme To This Object Only
- Make This Theme The Database Default

When you apply a theme to a specific object, Access lists this theme in the In This Database group in the Themes gallery. A ScreenTip identifies which object a theme applies to or whether a theme applies to the database.

See Also For information about modifying the font and color schemes for a theme and the steps you follow to create a custom theme, see section 4.3, "Format forms."

➤ **To apply a theme to a report**

1. In the Navigation pane, right-click the report, and then click **Layout View** or **Design View**.
2. On the **Report Design Tools Design** tool tab (or the **Report Layout Tools Design** tool tab), click **Themes**, and then select the theme you want to apply to the form.

Adding information to report headers and footers

In Layout view and Design view, you can use commands in the Design tool tab's Header/Footer group to insert standard elements in a report's header and footer sections. The Page Numbers command opens a dialog box in which you select a format, position, and alignment for page numbers. Page numbers appear in the Page Header or Page Footer section and can be centered or aligned at the left or right border. Clear the check box for the Show Number On First Page option to start pagination on the report's second page.

Use the Position options to specify
where page numbers will appear

The Logo, Title, and Date And Time commands add information to the Report Header section by default. You could add the date and time to the Page Header or Page Footer section by adding a text box control and then entering the expression *=Date() or =Time()*.

> **Tip** You can add other controls to a report's header or footer by dragging the appropriate control to that section of the form.

> ### To insert information in a report header or footer

1. In the Navigation pane, right-click the report, and then click **Design View** or **Layout View**.

2. On the **Report Design Tools Design** tool tab (or the **Report Layout Tools Design** tool tab), in the **Header/Footer** group, click the option for the element you want to add to the form.

   ○ **Logo** Select the image file from the **Insert Picture** dialog box.

   ○ **Title** Enter a title for the report in the label control that Access provides.

○ **Date and Time** Specify the date and time format you want to use in the **Date and Time** dialog box.

○ **Page Numbers** Specify the format, location (in the **Page Header** or **Page Footer** section), and alignment for report page numbers.

Adding backgrounds and images to a report

To use an image as the background for a report, click Background Image on the Report Design Tools Format tool tab (or the Report Layout Tools Format tool tab). Click Browse, and then open the location where the image file you want to use is stored.

After you add the background image, you should set properties to modify how Access displays it. Right-click the report and choose Report Properties. In the property sheet, click the Format tab. The properties you use to control the display of a background image include the following: Picture Type, Picture, Picture Tiling, Picture Alignment, and Picture Size Mode.

> **See Also** For detailed descriptions of these properties and their settings, see section 4.3, "Format forms."

You can also insert an image to provide a visual element to a report. On the Design tool tab in Layout view or Design view, click Insert Image. Select an image in the image gallery (which shows snapshots of images used on forms or other reports) or click Browse to open the Insert Picture dialog box, where you can locate the image file you want to include. Use the picture-related properties listed earlier in this topic to adjust how Access displays the image.

➤ **To add an image to a report background**

1. Open the report in Layout view or Design view.

2. Click the **Report Design Tools Format** tool tab (or the **Report Layout Tools Format** tool tab).

3. In the **Background** group, click **Background Image**.

4. Select an image in the **Image** gallery, or click **Browse** to open the **Insert Picture** dialog box to locate the image file you want to use.

5. On the **Report Design Tools Design** tool tab (or the **Report Layout Tools Design** tool tab), click **Property Sheet**, and then select **Report** in the **Selection Type** list.

6. On the property sheet's **Format** tab, specify settings for the **Picture Type, Picture, Picture Tiling, Picture Alignment,** and **Picture Size Mode** properties.

➤ **To add an image to a report**

1. Open the report in Layout view or Design view.

2. Click the **Design** tool tab.

3. In the **Controls** group, click **Insert Image**.

4. Select an image in the **Image** gallery, or click **Browse** to open the **Insert Picture** dialog box to locate the image file you want to use.

5. In the report, click where you want the image to appear.

6. On the **Design** tool tab, click **Property Sheet**. (Be sure the image is selected in the **Selection Type** list.)

7. On the property sheet's **Format** tab, specify settings for the **Picture Type, Picture, Picture Tiling, Picture Alignment,** and **Picture Size Mode** properties.

Applying page setup options

When a report is open in Design view or Layout view, the ribbon displays the Page Setup tool tab, which contains commands in two groups: Page Size and Page Layout. Use the commands in these groups to set page size and orientation, margins, and columns. You can also use the Page Setup dialog box to manage settings for these aspects of a report. Use the Page Setup dialog box when you want to apply custom settings instead of the standard settings Access provides.

The options for a report's page size include Letter (8.5 by 11 inches), A4 (8.27 by 11.69 inches), or Legal (8.5 by 14 inches). Choose the size you want to apply to the report from the options displayed on the Size menu in the Page Size group.

To adjust the margins for a report, click Margins in the Page Size group, and then choose one of the three options Access provides: Normal, Wide, and Narrow. You can refer to the dimensions Access lists and the simple preview to gauge how the margins affect the space provided for the data the report presents.

> **Tip** The Live Preview feature doesn't apply to margin settings, but if you display the report in Layout view, you can view the effect of each option on the report. Be sure to select the Show Margins check box in the Page Size group.

Select the Print Data Only option in the Size group if you want to print the report's data without the formatting applied to the report. To set the page orientation for the report, in the Page Layout group, select the Portrait or Landscape option.

If you want to set up a columnar report, click Columns in the Page Layout group, and then specify settings on the Columns tab in the Page Setup dialog box. You need to consider the number of fields, the width of report controls, and the page size when you set up a report in columns. Columnar reports are best used for lists, directories, or other types of reports that include only a few fields. Stacking the fields (by using the stacked layout, for example) can also save space.

Use the Grid Settings area to specify the number of columns and to set how much space appears between rows and columns. Adjust column dimensions by using the Width and Height boxes in the Column Size area. Select Same As Detail to fit the columns within the Detail section of the report. In the Column Layout area, click an option to indicate how the columns of data will be arranged.

The Page Setup dialog box also includes the Print Options and Page tabs. You can set specific dimensions for a report's margins on the Print Options tab instead of using the Normal, Wide, or Narrow option provided in the Page Size group. The Print Options tab also includes the Print Data Only check box.

The Page tab provides options also available in the Page Layout and Page Size groups, including the Portrait and Landscape options for the report's page orientation and page size settings. If you want Access to use printer settings for a printer other than the default printer specified for your computer, select Use Specific Printer, click Printer, and then specify the printer.

➤ **To specify page size settings for a report**

1. In the Navigation pane, right-click the report, and then click **Design View** or **Layout View**.

2. Click the **Report Layout Tools Page Setup** tool tab (or the **Report Design Tools Page Setup** tool tab).

3. In the **Page Size** group, click **Size**, and then click an option for the report's page size.

4. Click **Margins**, and then click one of the default options for page margins.

➤ **To specify page layout settings for a report**

1. In the Navigation pane, right-click the report, and then click **Design View** or **Layout View**.

2. Click the **Page Setup** tool tab.

3. In the **Page Layout** group, click **Portrait** or **Landscape** to set the page orientation.

4. Click **Page Setup** to open the **Page Setup** dialog box. Use the tabs in the dialog box to specify the following settings.

   ○ **Print Options tab** Set the page margins, and select **Print Data Only** if you want to apply this option.

   ○ **Page tab** Choose a paper size, and specify the printer to use to produce the report.

➤ **To specify column settings for a report**

1. In the Navigation pane, right-click the report, and then click **Design View** or **Layout view**.

2. Click the **Page Setup** tool tab.

3. In the **Page Layout** group, click **Columns**.

4. On the **Columns** tab in the **Page Setup** dialog box, specify the number of columns, the row and column spacing, the column size, and the column layout option, and then click **OK**.

5. Open the report in **Print Preview** to test the settings.

Adding calculated fields

In reports, you can use a calculated field to augment the information provided by the data fields. You can combine text fields by using the concatenation operator (the ampersand, &). For example, a calculated field of this type lets you display a contact's last name and first name in a single control.

[First Name] & " " & [Last Name]

You could also use the concatenation operator to create a custom label by using an expression such as the following:

="Please send your comments to " & [First Name]

To set up a calculated field, add a text box to the report, display the property sheet, and then click the ellipsis in the Control Source property to open the Expression Builder. Use the Expression Builder to add functions, operators, constants, and identifiers (which refer to the names of fields or tables, for example).

By using arithmetic operators, you can add, subtract, multiply, or divide the values in numeric fields. In a report that summarizes the amount spent in a specific budget category, divide that amount by the budget field to display the percentage spent of the total budget.

=Sum([AmountSpent])/[CampaignBudget]

As shown in the examples in this section, enclose identifiers such as field names in square brackets.

➤ **To create a calculated field**

1. Open the report in Design view or Layout view.

2. Add a text box control to the report, and then select that control.

3. On the **Report Design Tools Design** tool tab (or the **Report Layout Tools Design** tool tab), click **Property Sheet**.

4. On the property sheet's **Data** tab, click in the **Control Source** box, and then do one of the following.

   ○ Enter the expression that defines the calculated field directly in the **Control Source** box.

   ○ Press **Shift+F2** to open the **Zoom** dialog box, and enter the expression in the dialog box.

   ○ Click the ellipsis in the **Control Source** box to open the Expression Builder for help writing the expression.

Sorting records in a report

As you can for forms, you can use the Order By and Order By On Load properties to change the sort order for the records in a report without changing the sort order specified in its record source.

These properties appear on the Data tab in a report's property sheet. In the Order By property, enter the name of the field (enclosed in brackets) by which you want to sort the records. You can use more than one field by separating field names with a comma. By default, records are sorted in ascending order. Enter *DESC* after a field name to sort that field in descending order.

The setting you specify for the Order By property is saved with the report, but the sort order is not automatically applied when you open the report unless you set Order By On Load to Yes.

> **Tip** You can also specify the sort order for a report when you use the Report wizard, and in Layout view and Design view by using the Group & Sort command on the Report Design Tools Design tool tab (or the Report Layout Tools Design tool tab).

➤ **To set the Order By and Order By On Load properties**

1. Open the report in Design view or Layout view.

2. On the **Report Design Tools Design** tool tab (or the **Report Layout Tools Design** tool tab), in the **Tools** group, click **Property Sheet**.

3. On the property sheet's **Data** tab, click in the **Order By** property box, and then enter the name of the field or fields you want to sort by. Enclose the field names in brackets, and separate multiple field names with a comma. To sort in descending order, enter **DESC** after a field's name.

4. To sort the records when the form is opened, set **Order By On Load** to **Yes**.

Practice tasks

The practice files for these tasks are located in the MOSAccess2013\Objective5 practice file folder. You can save the results of the tasks in the same folder.

- Open the *Marketing_5* database.
- Open the *Campaign Summary* report in Layout view.
- Use the options in the *Page Size* and *Page Layout* groups to change the report's page orientation and the settings for its margins.
- Apply the Organic theme to the report. Create a custom color scheme for the report.
- Open the *Tasks* report in Design view. Create a field named *Task Duration* that calculates the difference between the start date and the due date.
- Create a report based on the *CampaignExpenses* table. Use the property sheet to sort the report by expense type.

Objective review

Before finishing this chapter, be sure you have mastered the following skills:

5.1 Create a report
5.2 Set report controls
5.3 Format reports

Index

About the author

 **John Pierce** was an editor and writer at Microsoft for 12 years. He is the author of *Microsoft Office Access 2003 Inside Track* (2004), with Paul Pardi; *MOS 2010 Study Guide for Microsoft Word Expert, Excel Expert, Access, and SharePoint Exams* (2011), with Geoff Evelyn; and *Team Collaboration: Using Microsoft Office for More Effective Teamwork* (2012), all published by Microsoft Press.

Now that you've read the book...

Tell us what you think!

Was it useful?
Did it teach you what you wanted to learn?
Was there room for improvement?

Let us know at http://aka.ms/tellpress

Your feedback goes directly to the staff at Microsoft Press,
and we read every one of your responses. Thanks in advance!